630-1 SWINNERTON. F Reflections from a village

Reflections
from a Village

Hutchinson
of London

FRANK SWINNERTON

Reflections
from a Village

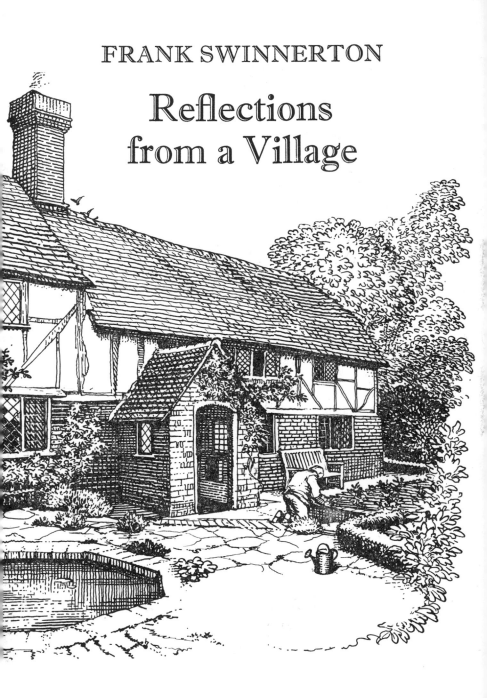

HUTCHINSON & CO (*Publishers*) LTD
178–202 Great Portland Street, London W1

London Melbourne Sydney
Auckland Bombay Toronto
Johannesburg New York

★

First published 1969

© Frank Swinnerton 1969
Decorations by J. S. Goodall
Design by Michael Brett

*This book has been set in Imprint, printed in Great Britain
on Antique Wove paper by Anchor Press, and
bound by Wm. Brendon, both of Tiptree, Essex*

09 095060 7

CONTENTS

PART THREE: *Old Residents*

Also by Frank Swinnerton

'To me a simple country-house, a nest,
is pleasanter than any palace, and, if
he be a King who lives in freedom and
according to his wishes, surely I am
King here.'

ERASMUS: *Convivium religiosum*

PART ONE
The Setting

ONE

The Village

OUR VILLAGE, which has a present population of six thousand, was long ago said to be the largest in England. Forty miles from London, but not on a main road, it is within thirty miles of the sea. Amid a network of lanes and winding roads, the single main street enjoys a strip of common land which for the past seventy years has been enriched by a magnificent double row of maple trees; and these trees, famous for miles around, are among our prides.

At its southern end the High Street forks, in one direction proceeding deviously south, between houses, but soon reaching rural landscape, the boundary of another county, and, finally, the English Channel. The left-hand fork, at something less than a right angle, meanders eastward through other villages and under the lee of the Surrey Hills, until it meets and is abruptly ended by an arterial road connecting London and the western extremity of England.

First yellow, and then exquisitely green in Spring, the maples change to a warm red, and afterwards to sepia. This, for them, is a time of glory; for the foliage has reached perfect maturity.

Later, when touched by frost, and swept from their branches by strong autumn winds, they shower the Common with a profusion of green, golden, and purple leaves. These, after heavy rain, may become treacherous for pedestrians; but before the rain, in their earlier crisp state, swirling waist-high in apparent stampede, they are exquisite. In conjunction with the oaks, beeches, and sycamores which simultaneously turn in our own garden, they recall, in miniature, the splendours of a New England Fall.

A small, quiet church, the original building of which is thought to date from the fourteenth century, lies near the High Street fork, half-hidden by elderly trees. Its stained-glass windows were lost in 1944, when much damage was caused by a flying bomb; but the church itself, however much it may have been restored in earlier years, remains a model of what such buildings should be, modest and satisfying to the eye. It is very well kept, with a square clock-adorned tower and porch; and among its curiosities is that carved drip-stone in the north transept representing the face of an extraordinary animal. This animal, by legend, is the very Cheshire Cat immortalised by Lewis Carroll in *Alice in Wonderland*.

I do not find the legend preposterous; for Lewis Carroll lived less than nine miles away, and just as he or Tenniel 'saw' the Ugly Duchess in the red chalk caricature at Windsor by one of Leonardo's pupils of an ugly old woman, so, in that still unfathomed treasure of nonsense (the Cat's question, 'did you say pig, or fig?' always seems to me its delicious acme), a stone head in our church may well have given the requisite hint to genius.

I offer no guarantee on this or any other point. I remark, however, as to the Church, which is dedicated to St Nicholas, that to see, after service, on a lovely summer evening, the loitering crowd of worshippers, each member of which, together with his or her life and character, is shrewdly known to the rest, is even now to recover the sort of past recorded by writers as diverse as Oliver Goldsmith, Miss Mitford, and Thomas Hardy. Just so must the villagers have loitered on Sundays long ago, before Simplicity was undermined by the Rational, and when a church was the unquestioned centre of communal life.

Was there such a time? I have lately been reading a number of books about the days of Erasmus, Luther, and Sir Thomas More; and the notion of an idyllic faith is not encouraged by the tales of a militant Pope leading his soldiers to war, of burnings, the rack, and disorderly monasteries. Perhaps there never was a 'merrie England', in which all were humbly devout? Perhaps there was always unrest and persecution, a battle for freedom of the mind against the tyrannies of authority? Perhaps I, a townsman by birth, always sentimentalised the country life?

I do not think this last can be true, for certain reasons which I will discuss later. I shall say here only that on our first arrival in the village I discovered how many, high and low, made a point of going regularly to church, and how many devout sects flourished in the neighbourhood. There was not only the village church I have described but a modern, red-brick auxiliary church, dedicated to St Andrew, which stood rather bleakly on the edge of the Common, overlooking a football pitch. There were also churches or chapels for a considerable number of Roman Catholics, Methodists, and Baptists; together with smaller conventicles for Seventh Day Adventists, Plymouth Brethren, and—I was told—members of the now moribund Countess of Huntingdon's Connection.

As will be seen from this list, our village was miscellaneously religious. One of the first names I heard pronounced, not with awe, but with a sort of amused respect, was that of a former rector, an archdeacon, who, with a contemporaneous doctor, stood higher in the social hierarchy than a couple of landed baronets still benevolently a part of village life. But the Church of England was not all-powerful. There was a strong element of Nonconformity among the shopkeepers; and the Nonconformists resisted until the last moment an inevitable secularisation of Sunday. For them, Sunday was the Lord's Day; and should be kept for worship. This is a good English tradition.

However, the days immediately following the First World War held many changes, one of which involved a relaxation of manners. And it says a great deal for the natural tolerance of villagers that as the changes came no quarrels occurred. Men and women pursued their own ways, did their utmost to preserve ancient standards, and seemed to be happy in their faith. Nor did any of them show inquisitiveness about what my wife and I believed or did not believe.

I assume that all this represented a survival of nineteenth-century liberalism, and am confirmed in my supposition that, whatever violences of persecution there may have been for centuries among clamorous theologians, simple folk preserved the essentials of universal charity. The reason? They took life as they found it, bothered little about niceties of creed, worked too hard from morning until night to indulge in the bigotries of self-tormenting dogmatists, and—it is an essential for peaceable co-existence—sought no dominance over others.

TWO

Village Folk

NOT VERY far from our immediate district lies the original home of cricket as a national game. It is not surprising, therefore, that when the High Street broadens at its northern end into an old-style Common, on which a fair is held several times a year, it should embrace, as neighbouring Commons do, a cricket green.

This green, fringed with limes as well as sparser maples, reveals some of the oldest cottages in the village, two of them at least, including our own, dating from the early seventeenth century; and on its sward some of the greatest cricketers in the world have played and still play against our village team. When they do so, the district is *en fête*; two or three thousand sit around the field on improvised supports; and local pride is warmly stimulated.

Jutting hills to east and west, and Downs to the south, catch most of the winds and flying storms, so that, being in a sort of land bay, we enjoy mainly quiet and dry weather. Only gales directly from the south-west drench us, and gales from the south-east, which remind us of the mistral in Southern France, pierce our walls. When these south-easters carry snow, they sometimes beat up under the tiles and stain our otherwise staunch bedroom ceilings. These winds are killers.

As for transport, there was from 1865 until just the other day a single pair of lines which carried rail traffic between junctions no more than nine and thirteen miles away. The short trains, sometimes pushed from behind by steam-driven engines, could not leave our station until the driver had been handed an iron instrument resembling a mace, which governed the next stretch of line; and if two trains were in the station at the same time it was amusing to watch the exchange of these instruments, without which no traffic could proceed. Few passengers travelled by the train, most of them being known to each other, if only by sight; and their conversation, on politics, literature, and civilisation in general, was high-toned and dogmatic. I have heard many literary statements, perhaps directed at myself, of a most preposterous nature. And as the men talked the train ambled peacefully through wide and beautiful meadows, at one point past two of the most exquisite weeping willows I ever saw, as if it wished to give everybody a panoramic view of the county.

When we first came to the village, more than forty years ago, a windmill stood on the Common, beyond almost idle cross-roads. The cricket field was rolled and mown by an old man who walked beside a docile elderly horse; and he was always, in daylight, wet or shine, to be seen at work. The field was his joy, his hobby, his never-ending preoccupation. It responded to his efforts as a good field should do. Visiting cricketers always said his pitches were the best they knew. His name, a good Surrey name, was Stemp.

Every morning and evening a flock of unsuperintended geese set out on, or returned from, an adventurous journey in search of food. They exchanged querulous remarks, and sometimes hissed at passing children; but beyond holding up a little traffic did no harm. One, which had been lame from birth, and there-

16

fore, as a gosling, had been used to much petting, went out with the rest and was away all day. On reaching home, however, it separated from the rest and turned in at a doorway leading to the owner's kitchen. If the owner's two cats, as often happened, were snoozing side by side in front of the fire, it pushed in between them as a matter of course.

Every morning and evening, also, a small herd of cows made a rather similar excursion and return, in charge of a devoted cowman. It is common knowledge that in every herd there is one cow which takes the lead; and in this case the leader was a shrewd old character named Rosie. One day the cowman, who had fallen behind in conversation with a friend, suddenly noticed that his charges were far ahead. Dismayed, he did the only possible thing. Stumbling after them at a gallop, he shouted breathlessly: 'Rosie! Rosie! To the *left*, Rosie!' Rosie turned to the left; the others followed. All was well.

Rosie's owner kept bees, which flew to considerable distances in search of honey. We often saw and heard them in a very fine pyrus japonica which grew up the front of our cottage; but their range was wide and they usually went back to their hives laden with pollen from far away. One afternoon, however, we noticed a considerable buzzing inside the dining-room windows, and were astonished to find many bees clustered on the leaded panes and in some cases lying on their backs on the window-sills. Having given what help I could, I shut the windows; and afterwards, meeting the farmer, I mentioned the odd happening.

'What was the matter with your bees the other afternoon?' I asked. 'They were straying indoors, and didn't seem able to find their way out again.'

He threw his shoulders back and swayed from side to side. 'Can't make it out,' said he. 'They were straggling home all anyhow; and trying to get into the wrong hives. Fighting. There were horrible battles.'

The ground before the hives had been littered with dead bees. It was a mystery to all; for although the battles subsided there were odd bees crawling disconsolately among the corpses for hours afterwards.

Only three or four days later was the explanation of this extraordinary happening found. It was the Demon Drink. Some neighbours a quarter of a mile away had been turning out the lees of their elderberry wine. Homeward-bound bees paused to investigate, took one sip and then another. When stumbling into our dining-room to rest awhile, or bumbling into hives that were not their own, they were completely intoxicated.

Another old farmer whom we knew only by sight was said to be a grumpy old man. He always wore a discoloured straw boater and I think a stuffing of cotton-wool in each ear. Driving past in a horse-drawn trap or dog-cart he would flourish his whip with the greatest geniality; and I do not believe that he was at all grumpy. We discovered, however, in him an instance of one of the burning questions of country life—that of hedges and boundaries. Just as the sober bees resented the territorial intrusions of their tipsy fellows, and fought them, so very peaceable men are filled with rage at the sight of other peaceable men, as they think, trespassing.

The old farmer defended his land. Two other men, and one of them unquestionably a darling, but both stubborn, crossed each other in this same question—whether a hedge should be trimmed by one or his neighbour. The quarrel became so acute that they went to war (or law) over the boundary. They were told by the judge that they were silly children who should have known better; and were fined half-a-crown apiece.

We had no hedge troubles. If a hedge was claimed by one of the cottagers we were complaisant. Indeed, we found that this question of 'property' arose only if it was thought that some scheme of grab was afoot; and as we were not grabbers we were soon accepted as friends. Favourable accounts passed from mouth to ear. It was natural to them to speak without hesitation to strangers. We went for long walks in the afternoons, sometimes accompanied by rambling dogs in search of congenial companionship; and when we did this we never troubled to lock doors. We learned the paths of the district, largely instructed by an old solicitor with a wilderness-garden, whose hobby it was to preserve all rights of way. This man had the whole history of the village and the district in his head; and was willing to share it. He was never in a hurry. He was very tall, and his manner was abrupt; but he gave us plants from his wilderness, and told many curious stories. He was the first member of the Parish Council with whom I conversed intimately.

Our postmen, who took weekly turns in delivery, were both 'characters'. One, who managed his round at a regular pace, would make, hardly pausing, cheerful but depressive comparisons between his own garden troubles and ours. 'I see you're same as me,' he said. 'Greenfly and them old cuckoo spit.' He never gossiped, and his appearances were regular to the minute. The other, more wayward, and therefore less punctual, was very tiny, with a treble voice, a bulging brow, and philosophic eyes which gave the impression of being out of alignment. He was entirely dwarfed by his big letter-bag; and his progress through the village was hindered by encounters with many friends. Everybody stopped him; if he saw a man hurrying to catch a train he would always dive into his bag for the letter or letters which he thought might need immediate attention; and in this way he did me, as he did others, many an innocent kindness.

His preferred companions were little boys, for whom he bought sweets, and whom he took to see films in a curious shed which was then our only place of general entertainment. It was run as pastime by a local tobacconist who could be found in his shop mending the rather battered films with stamp-edging before showing them in the evening; and our little postman was a constant patron with his train of children. This postman was universally known as 'Old John'. He was very conscientious. With his innocent friendliness and piping ancient voice and affable noddings, he might have come straight from a fairy tale.

19

John was not the only character in a village which was still so far away from sophistication that it continued to breed individuals and be amused by simple things. There were others, his juniors, who outlasted him and passed bravely into a newer world, still full of reminiscence and twinkling humour.

From these men, whether they came to the cottage to work or were encountered in the village itself, I heard many a tale, told without malice, but with that relish for the misfortunes of others which salts the more accomplished recitals of the Night Watchman invented by W. W. Jacobs.

One such story was of an ancient man of the cloth whom I never saw, but whose reputation for piety was hardly to be paralleled. He, seeking to fell a small tree, misjudged its reaction, and tumbled on his back, speaking words, and confessing otherwise hidden disasters, which those who heard them could hardly credit and would never repeat. Another was of an old man who went to the doctor to complain that rheumatism had entirely wrecked his right shoulder. 'I can't lift me arm no higher than this, Doctor,' said he, showing how it would not rise above the level of his chest. 'And last week (suiting the action to the word) 'I could get it right over my head—like this!'

A third, related with complacent chuckles by one who had been there, was of a naughty workman who, engaged with his mates on certain repairs to an unoccupied house, covetously noticed among certain debris an alarm clock which he thought would make a brave addition to his own home. His mates, however, being as sharp-eyed as he, not only saw the clock but saw what he did with it. They watched him slip the treasure into his carpet bag, along with tools, tea-can, and other kit.

Instead of taking a high moral line, they mischievously waited until he was absent for a few minutes, wound the clock, and set the alarm for the very hour at which they would all be trooping homeward down the house's steep drive. Sure enough, they were only half-way down the drive when a terrible, unstoppable din arose from the rascal's bag. He was utterly confounded, while they pretended astonishment. In the end, satisfied with a good and salutary deed, they went off in excellent spirits, leaving him to ponder the old saying, 'Be sure your sin will find you out!'

A fourth story was less merry. I repeat it because it demonstrates the reverse side of simplicity. A hale old man who worked at the corn chandlers' was talking about things he recalled, and his companions thought if he remembered such things, which had happened long before, he must be getting old. How old was he? 'I d'know,' said he. 'Suppose I might be seventy.' 'Then,' they told him, 'you ought to have your Old Age Pension. It's worth it. You just find out how old you are.' They helped him to do so; and he found that he was not seventy, but eighty. The shock was so great that, convinced of his hopeless antiquity, he instantly took to his bed, from which he never rose again.

Such was the result of innocence. Nor must I forget to mention at this point that when we first arrived in the village we found shopkeepers carrying on business as they must have done while Queen Victoria was alive. Needing a very large envelope, I called on one of them, a stationer, mild, hesitant, spectacled, and, I discovered, a gifted extemporiser in chapel. He produced exactly what I wanted. 'Splendid!' said I. 'How much?' His reply was: 'They're four a penny, sir; or two for a ha'penny. Or you *could* have one for a farthing.'

I felt I had not been mistaken in my dream of idyllic life in the English countryside.

THREE

Diversion to London

MY WIFE and I are both London born and bred, a fact which assures us of a common outlook. The Londoner, in his ignorance of what lies beyond his own city, may be the most provincial of all beings; but Henry James said of London: 'You may call it dreary, heavy, stupid, dull, inhuman, vulgar at heart and tiresome in form. . . . It is the biggest aggregation of human life—the most complete compendium of the world.' This remains true.

James made no comment, as far as I know, on the Londoner as a type. That would have been beyond the power even of his wonderfully subtle mind; and I should not like to attempt any analysis. Nor could I indulge any vainglorious thoughts, in spite of contacts with its citizens during Hitler's bombing attacks, when danger was acute all day and every night. No, the only generalisation I shall venture is that the Londoner is bred to unimpressible irony. His irony is free from bitterness; it is occasionally witty; its chief feature is good-humoured derision for the self-importance of other men.

It was a Londoner who, on being told a boastful story of

achievement by a more *naif* character, responded drily: 'And then you woke up,' meaning that he did not believe a word of the story. It was another Londoner who, still expressing incredulity, first used the phrase, 'Yus I don't fink.' Not for him, unless he is a Charles Lamb, to extol the place of his birth: conviction of its supremacy in the world and in world history, never expressed in coloured phrase, lies deep in his being. He leaves the paeans to such provincial settlers as Dr Johnson and Jim Bone; and the reproduction of his manners is to be found at its best in the pages of a South African writer, Neil Lyons, whose coffee-stall conversations should immortalise *Arthur's, A London Lot, A Market Bundle,* and other neglected master works.

Nevertheless, Londoners understand each other. They have this common outlook, to which I have referred; and my wife and I share it. There is a difference between us. She is of South London (that is to say, born in London south of the river Thames), and I am of the North. In North London, for some reason, there has always been an assurance of superiority to southerners. We, Swinnertons included, thought of them as people living at a lower geographical level, and therefore almost submerged in primeval dimness.

Whether this belief originated in the fact that the original walled City was on the North Bank of the Thames, while all the noble houses, once their owners left the City, stretched westward along the northern bank known for centuries as the Strand, I cannot say; but as Southerners could never by any chance have heard Bow Bells they obviously were not authentic Cockneys. The tides of a great river lay between them and that celebrated carillon. We said, like the singer in *The Belle of New York*, 'Of course you can never be like us. But be as like us as you are able to be.' Yes, yes, they were a sort of Londoners; but I remember that when, in a novel, I described a family living in Kennington Park my brother's comment was: 'Of course, they're all really North Londoners!'

In this arrogance, we took no heed of the fact that the Globe

Theatre of Shakespeare's glory was in Southwark, which gentry and groundlings reached by small boat. Even if we acknowledge the Globe, we considered that Southwark had only been reclaimed for culture by one theatre, and afterwards from a featureless desert by Henry Thrale's brewery. Johnson's visits to Streatham, where the Thrales had a country villa, were made in search of good fare; his true home was in Fleet Street. And although there was Greenwich, down the river, the Crystal Palace at Sydenham, and a school, not unknown to fame, at Dulwich, these places were of small account. The typical South London suburb was Tooting, which was as much a name of common ridicule in music-halls as Wigan.

My wife did not know this. I have never enlightened her. After all, we have made our common home in Surrey, a broad county, full of beauty, on the southern side of the Thames. Furthermore, my own memories of Wood Green, where I was born, and such other northern suburbs as Hornsey, East Finchley, and Hampstead, where I lived from time to time in boyhood, are now dim. The places are probably so much changed that I should feel a stranger in any of them. And to raise so invidious a distinction between the places of our origin, especially as my wife has childhood memories of St Albans, which is twenty miles north of the Thames, would be to risk challenges which I strive in all circumstances to avoid.

We both recall London as it was in the past, and care less for the current city, with its up-rearing piles of flats, where dwellers twenty floors above the street are frightened by their remoteness from company and, after taking children to school, hesitate to re-ascend to their model kitchens. Nor do we enjoy visits to old haunts, where the multiple stores garishly jostle each other and all supply the same tinned and packaged goods with distressing uniformity. The London we knew as children was a place of romance.

In my own case it was very nearly the same as the London of Charles Dickens. Life there had changed very little in fifty years; and Dickens, for all that superfine critics speak of him as a vulgar dealer in melodrama and pantomime, was a realist who knew the town. He, and the actors in pantomime harlequinades, reproduced what was in fact the natural comedy of a rough and ready system in which the poor took their chances, and lived from day to day.

They were indeed poor; but there were compensations, especially for the young, for whom so small a sum as the now-vanished farthing (sometimes shoppers were given a packet of pins instead of a farthing change) could buy exquisite treats. These ranged, in my recollection, from minute oval wooden boxes of sugar containing little tin spoons to delicious squares of toasted coconut, and from bags of yellow acid- or rosy peardrops to black and white striped bullseyes, dry chewing sticks called locusts, and black licorice laces. The problem was always of how long the individual sweet could be made to last.

There were always the ice cream or hokey-pokey men, always Italians, with their brightly coloured barrows and a swarm of youngsters engaged in cajolery—'Gi's a taster, Jack!'— because they had no ha'pennies; and the hurdy-gurdy men who turned the handles of organs on a stick, while fezzed and coated monkeys scrambled about on the pavement or perched on the instrumentalist's shoulder.

The streets were gas-lit, so that dark corners abounded. So did altogether unlighted alleyways into which strange seedy men vanished as they did in *Oliver Twist* or *Little Dorrit*. Such men were also to be glimpsed in daylight; and one day my mother, taking a short cut from Clerkenwell Road, and carrying a little open-topped bag of raffia, down a narrow street called Saffron Hill, escaped the loss of the bag's contents because a would-be thief, plunging his hand into the bag, speared himself on the upturned points of a large pair of scissors, and ran away screaming.

Butchers stood outside their shops chanting 'Buy, buy, buy!' and were challenged by rivals across the street who shouted 'Lovely! Lovely!' The meat they sold was often blackened by

25

exposure; but nobody minded. There were no refrigerators, and no inspectors to take particulars or test scales or pry into dark recesses behind the shops; and little boys hung about as Dickens's urchins did, watching every chance to appropriate dropped money or ill-wrapped parcels, or even fragments of meat which had fallen from the butchers' knives.

A correspondent, after reading an article I had written about Clerkenwell, recalled glorious days in Exmouth Street, when such opportunist boys had a golden harvest. The grocer, of whom my mother dealt, had a termagant wife, who was apt, when in a temper, to make scenes in his shop. Her voice carried far, and the lurking boys, hearing it, hurried near. They were sure of the amusement a row always gave them. They hoped for something more.

It came. First there was the loud shouting, then a screaming as hysteria approached, and finally a cascade of tins which the wife had aimed at her husband. They were flung with such force that some of them came right through the open doorway and into the gutter. This was what the loitering urchins had expected. They pounced in joy; and having been 'artful dodgers' from their earliest years they were gone in a twinkling.

In such conditions London held much unhappiness; and as in the poorer districts there was almost universal squalor, so there must have been an unconscionable amount of misery. But Somerset Maugham, comparing notes with me, once said that he had just revisited friends whom he had known in medical student days. The family was still living in the neighbourhood of St Thomas's Hospital: but whereas in the past, cramped and oppressed in dingy lodgings, they had been jokers who made light of all their troubles, they had become, in new palatial quarters, embarrassingly full of discontent. As was his habit, Maugham drew no conclusion; he merely stated what he had noticed. His attitude continued to be that of the man who wrote *Of Human Bondage*, who said of the Hospital: 'There was neither good nor bad there. There were just facts. It was life.'

Dickensian London—and the London of my childhood—was certainly in some of its aspects repulsive. It was very dirty. The women's long skirts picked up abounding mud and dust. This same dust penetrated all clothes, the hair (much less often washed and treated than it is now), the skin. Food was exposed to every March wind and November fog; horse manure, uncontrolled street refuse, and smoking chimneys produced an atmosphere almost as evil as that of today's petrol fumes. Henry James made a list of the town's horrors, including its darkness and its ugliness, before he declared it to be the greatest compendium of human life ever known; and what he said in 1881, eleven years after Dickens's death, was true.

Dickens knew it all, by heart. He walked recklessly about the city, by day and night, into all the alleys, by all the dark abysses beside the river; and the rich drama of his novels was reality seasoned and exaggerated by an exuberant fancy. His critics see and condemn only the fancy; with greater penetration they would recognise the truth on which fancy built.

FOUR

'Get Him into the Country'

THAT GROCER'S shop, as I have said, stood in Clerken-well, the scene of Arnold Bennett's more decorous and intensive study *Riceyman Steps*. I knew the district so well in childhood that I can still find my way about it. My mother's father, a Scotsman (he was affectionately known, and signed himself, as 'Grumps', to distinguish him from the Stafford-shire-born Swinnerton grandfather, who was always 'the Old Chap' or 'the Old Chap at City Road') lived in one of the big houses, still standing, in Farringdon Road, north of what is now Rosebery Avenue. The house then faced the high walls surrounding Coldbath House of Correction, which was de-molished to make room for Mount Pleasant Parcels Post Office; and it was in this house that I had my first of two narrow escapes from death by illness.

The illness was diphtheria. I was eight years old; and I should have died but for my mother's nursing. She and I were isolated from the rest of the family in a room at the top of the house behind a heavily-disinfected brown blanket; and she fought possible infection by taking potash tablets, the like of which cannot now be bought. The reason for their withdrawal from sale is apparently that they ignite when carried loose in a man's pocket; but as proprietary substitutes are inferior it is just as well that inoculation has made the disease rare.

I remember the look and smell of the blanket, and the hot sense of fever within myself; otherwise I have only one reminiscence. It is that as my throat had to be painted daily, and the doctor had an abominable habit of using a spoon to press down my tongue, I very artfully on one occasion pretended to be fast asleep. The performance was successful. Unfortunately, just as he was going, it occurred to the doctor to say: 'I wonder if he'd wake up if I gave him a penny.' I could not restrain a giggle; and the spoon followed as usual.

At last I was thought to be completely well again; and my aunt Lily, a younger sister of my mother's, took me to Brighton for the sea air. Even in those days this magnificent town was known as 'Doctor Brighton'. Alas, one day when my aunt and I were walking over the cliffs towards Rottingdean, watching and listening to the skylarks overhead, something terrible happened. I stumbled with the onset of diptheretic paralysis. I have a faint memory of Lily's consternation; none at all of the dismal return to Farringdon Road.

'You must get him into the country,' said the doctor. 'He must have fresher air than this.' And so, not immediately, but as soon as arrangements could be made, our little family deserted Grumps and Clerkenwell, and removed to Hornsey, in North London, not very far from my birthplace. Even then, Hornsey was not quite 'country'; but there was little traffic there, and little smoke, so that the atmosphere was unpolluted.

As far as my health was concerned, the move was very successful. At first I was largely confined to the house, where I invented games such as a hobbler could play, and read many books. As time passed, however, I received many kindnesses from neighbours and others. One of these neighbours, a little Scotch girl named Liza, is still alive, and writes to me from time to time. Another benefactor was a milkman named Charlie Davis, who took me riding, almost daily, in his backless float, where we stood side by side behind a brown, fast-trotting pony called Tom. Tom knew all the houses where he was given lumps of sugar, and outside these would advance on to the pavement, scrabbling with one of his forelegs in plea and expectation. He was never struck with a whip. Charlie simply said 'Come on,' and gave the reins a little twitch. Then we were away. It was a wonderful sensation, enabling me ever afterwards to imagine what it was like in Roman days to ride in a chariot.

I also became a passenger whenever my wicker-seated go-cart was borrowed for use as a stage-coach by my brother and his friends, who played bushrangers or Red Indians in Highgate Woods, a couple of miles away. The Woods, full of steep, suddenly turning paths among dense undergrowth, were ideal for surprises; and although I do not remember ever being thrown out the go-cart had some rough usage. Other children of my own age, including Liza and her brother Rob, played with me. And, month by month, although often ill, with bouts of headache and sickness, I grew stronger. In about two years the paralysis disappeared, never to return.

FIVE

The Cottage
is Found

THAT IS the end of an autobiographical digression, which
appears because during those difficult years I had a
dream. It was of a day far in the future when I should live in
the real country, in a cottage of my own. A dream common
enough among town-dwellers, and in my own case probably as
sentimental as it often proves. I did not want grandeur; I
wanted, in the words of Jasper Petulengro, 'Sun, moon, and
stars, bròther. And likewise the wind on the heath.'

My London experience had been of back-yards and those
squares of asphalt attached to 'buildings'. At Hornsey our
'garden' was a small patch of battered earth between fences,
rendered smaller by a high bank where all was shadowed by a
spreading may tree. It contained no flower-beds, no flowers.

I had, however, in pre-diphtheric days, enjoyed one glorious
shock. I was six, and for some reason was walking homewards
alone from the Home and Colonial Infants' School near King's
Cross station. It was a Spring afternoon; and the walk took me
past a familiar greengrocer's shop on the corner of a side street.
In that side street was an overwhelming display of cut hyacinths,

pink, white, and blue. The open window was full of them, massed, head to head, for what must have been a width of seven or eight and a height of quite four feet; and to my juvenile eye and nostrils they represented a mountain of colour and an intoxication of scent.

I have never forgotten this happening. Nearly eighty years afterwards memory of it returns every time I see hyacinths in bloom; and while I now greatly prefer other flowers, and find hyacinths hard and too heavily scented, I cannot resist them. They represent a first discovery of floral beauty.

Another memory is of periodical visits to Brighton; and especially of what seemed to be a regular enforced stop at signals outside some unidentified country railway station (could it have been Hassocks?), where the lovely green contours of the South Downs stretched far and wide, and where skylarks were ever rising higher and higher into a cloudless blue. When, beside these enchantments, I heard in exquisite silence the soft hissing of the engine—tf, tf, tf—my feeling was one of rapture.

At first, of course, I had no worldly ambition at all. Sensations were everything. It was when I began to write little stories and produce a miniature hand-written domestic magazine that the dream lost vagueness. It then became as positive as the materialistic man's determination to achieve wealth and power.

Circumstances dictated that I should continue for nearly thirty years more to live in London; but before we were married my wife and I put our heads together and resolved that we would both, as far as possible, give up urban life and find a cottage set in a garden full of flowers. For as Bacon said, 'God *Almightie* first planted a *Garden*. And indeed, it is the Purest of Humane pleasures.'

We nearly missed our cottage. After a vain hunt in several counties, I put my problem to a West End firm of house agents. They listened attentively; and at last sent me a sheaf of papers describing perhaps twenty cottages. They said: 'We particularly draw your attention to Old Tokefield, Cranleigh, Surrey.'

'Particular attention!' There must be reasons. 'Strange,' quoth I, as Laurence Sterne said when the word 'France' produced such an effect upon 'my gentleman'. 'I'll look into them.'

I did so. I made a railway journey which brought me to the village later in the day than I intended. I then received my first blow; for when I asked for the cottage by name nobody recognised it. 'Who lives there?' I did not know. Afterwards I realised that, in a place where houses register locally by the name of their occupiers, only postmen know that Mrs Town lives at 'Mon Repos' and Mrs Gown at 'Dunromin'. The matter was complicated by a further difficulty. What was now called 'Old Tokefield' had previously been 'Holly Tree Cottage' and 'Sunset Cottage'.

A second shock followed half-an-hour later, when at last I found somebody who hesitated.

'Oh,' said he. 'Is that where the artist lives?'

'It might be,' was my cautious reply.

He waved a hand, murmuring:

'Well, I don't exactly know; but you might try over there. Them holly trees.'

I followed the direction of his wave, and, as policemen say, 'proceeded'. But in nearing the holly trees I saw a tall man emerge from a gate between them, and stride away.

He was dressed in a tremendous sombrero hat, a brown velvet jacket, and gaiters. I stopped dead. This was the type of costume I had always associated with self-conscious amateur artists and olde arty-crafty preciousness; and I was a confirmed professional who, like other professionals in that age—Wells, Bennett, Galsworthy, Maugham, and men of my own generation,—dressed as other men did, some of them even wearing bowler hats. All I could see of the cottage behind some tall hedges was its tiled roof, casement windows, and half-timbered front. What if Old Tokefield should be 'olde' and 'quaint'? What if it should be some gimcrack reproduction or white elephant? The prospect was highly daunting. I turned tail. This, evidently, was not the unpretentious cottage I had envisaged.

I had been charmed, however, by the maple trees and by a group of warrantably genuine old cottages at the roadside. The cricket field, also, was a tremendous lure to a cricket-lover. I scented in these surroundings leisure, and tranquillity, the very things I needed. And as, driven by the need to catch my return train to London very quickly, I hurried to the railway station I caught sight of the premises of some local agents who, as it proved, worked in conjunction with my London benefactors. I entered.

'Have you anything else in the village?' I asked. 'A fake artist seems to live in the place I came to see.'

'Oh, he's a real artist,' replied the agent. He then named Lawson Wood, celebrated for his posters and admirable comic drawings of animals.

'Ah!' said I. 'I did him an injustice. All right; it's too late to go back to the house. I'm engaged this evening. I'll drive down, with my *fiançée*, next Sunday.'

I then owned a rather bulbous little car, which was going fast if it touched thirty miles an hour. At that speed it bounced from side to side of the road. But in those days I was a bolder driver than I am now, and had no fear of Sunday traffic. The journey was made. Lawson Wood, who confessed that his ambition was to withdraw from all distracting society and become a serious landscape painter, proved to be a most likeable man, with a charming wife and three equally charming children. His clothes, towards which I had shown such lamentable prejudice, were worn without affectation, because he was a countryman by birth, and found them comfortable; while his manner was as gentle and direct as anybody could wish. Also, he had the candour of the professional artist in talking to another professional—a class (I mean the artists) which I have always found outstandingly alert in observation.

He showed us the cottage, his big garden studio, his pictures, and such furniture as he was willing to sell. He at once became our friend, as he remained until his death a few years ago. He talked eloquently, and explained that the conversion of old cottages was his hobby, which he indulged without hoping to make large profits, but because the planning of houses and gardens gave him extreme pleasure.

I restrained my own tendency to chatter. My wife-to-be, never talkative except to myself, said not a word. We learned afterwards that we had disconcerted Wood by what he thought our oyster-like lack of enthusiasm; but in fact our speechlessness had been the result of deep feeling. In the car, as we drove away, we exchanged meaningful nods. With the optimism of inexperience, we had both decided that the cottage represented our ideal, and we were determined to possess it.

We were not wrong. Nor were we wrong about the village, for the reason that we knew nothing about it. Being Londoners, with no experience of life in a small community, we ignored the implications of residence among those who would expect us to take an active part in their own social activities. We did not want callers. We did not want to exchange dinner parties. We had plenty of friends elsewhere; and, as I was told a few years ago by a reflective writer, I am 'an odd mixture of the sociable and the reclusive'. In this instance the reclusive was dominant.

Indeed, I remembered with sympathy those characters in Conan Doyle's early novel, *The Mystery of Cloomber*, who set up a notice by their front gate which read: 'General and Mrs Heatherstone have no wish to increase the circle of their acquaintance.' The General was a very eccentric man indeed, who had Indian holy men on his trail. I was not equally eccentric. Therefore we set up no notice, and a few people took it for granted that as writing can be done, almost instinctively, and certainly without labour, at any time, visits in morning, afternoon, or evening would be in order. As a consequence we had some early embarrassments. When it was realised that I worked all day and every day (as I still do), understanding developed and cordiality became the rule.

After a few months we had survived all strangeness. It was reported to us that one day, after my wife had left his shop, one old trader exclaimed 'That's the nicest lady in the village!' And while for a few years it was believed among the ancients that, like Lawson Wood, I was a painter, my sedentary occupation was not held against me. In fact we had fallen among kind and good-humoured people, who to this day, whatever the changes, losses, and acquisitions from elsewhere, remain kind and good-humoured. This fact proves that the English, when not badgered by politicians nor hardened by over-sophistication, are, as they have always been, the most naturally civilised people in the world.

SIX

Settling In

O UR NEW home was on two floors, a long, low, half-timbered dwelling, with a big almost square central chimney and a tiled roof. It dated, roughly, from the year 1600, and had been converted by Lawson Wood and his architect friend John Clarke from three small cottages, one of four rooms, the others of two rooms apiece. These latter must have been small, and very low ceilinged; for our tiled dining-room, newly sunk below street level by a depth of two steps to give it reasonable height, had been contrived from the living-rooms of both.

In spite of the sunken floor, tall men needed, as they still need, to beware of striking their heads against the beams. Fortunately, although not short, I never had any knocks; but I remember that when Aldous Huxley and Robert Nichols, who were both over six feet, arrived together to pay a call their apprehensive crouching whenever they crossed the room kept us amusedly anxious during the entire visit. They, I think, were our tallest callers; and even to them no mishap occurred. Their private sensations and after-comments were never revealed;

but as both remained our friends until they died these cannot have been very severe.

Other valuable heads—although it is true that Arnold Bennett did knock his in the scullery doorway—have been in less obvious danger; and nobody has ever suffered from claustrophobia under our roof. The upstairs ceilings are satisfactorily high, and there are plenty of casement windows which, as they face directly south, admit air, and all possible sunshine.

Besides a built-on kitchen there are three rooms and—I must reveal as something which purists may condemn—a bathroom on the ground floor. Of these three, in addition to the dining-room, one is a parlour which we still call 'the nursery', while the other is my wife's tiny sitting-room, where there is space for not much more than a couple of chairs, her piano, bureau, and personal bookcases. This is a very bright and cheerful place.

When we inspected the cottage it was full of antique furniture. Some of this was good, even noble; but the total effect was too museum-like for a pair of unsophisticated home-makers. We sat, for lunch, on oaken forms at a long refectory table; and the only armchair we noticed was an old bare-seated grandfather. I was done with grandfathers, and forms, and refectory tables. I had experienced them in the past.

Four bedrooms, two large (one with an additional dormer window in the grand steep north-facing roof) and two small, completed the accommodation. Only two of the rooms shared a landing; the others were reached by separate staircases, all of old oak and as slippery as ice.

Only forty years later, when, by the kindness of one of the village's admirable solicitors, we were enabled to study some of the old deeds and conveyances, did we realise something of the history of our new home. We had been told that the original structure was Elizabethan; but we knew nothing of a long tale of successive owners. These could be traced through references to tenements and cottages, gardens, and common rights, back as far as the reign of George III; and several familiar village names, the bearers of which are alive today, figured as those of former owners and conveyors.

The gap between Queen Elizabeth and the eighteenth century was unfilled. All that the oldest conveyance indicated was that part of the property was 'formerly Elizabetha Tokefield's'. Who Elizabetha Tokefield could have been, nobody knew. Nevertheless her name appeared, more than once, as the ancient owner. Hence the name given by Lawson Wood to the converted cottages, 'Old Tokefield'; and under this our own purchase was described. It remains to this day, cut in the front gate.

Having acquired our home, we were confronted with the problem of furnishing it; and as we proposed to live long within its walls we resolved to make as comfortable a home (according to our notions of comfort) as possible. Two armchairs in what we call the dining-room, which in effect is the living-room, were essential. But others, besides ourselves, would wish to sit at ease; therefore we bought further armchairs and an enormous soft-cushioned settee which made its entrance to the room only through the genius of its bearers. I still do not know how they performed this feat. The settee's exit will call for similar genius; but I gladly leave the matter to posterity. I doubt if I shall be here.

Other furniture, sometimes of oak, and sometimes of mahogany, came from the same distinguished source. It was all unpretentious; but in our opinion it was beautiful. A few mistakes were made through my ignorance. Most of them have been rectified; what bore the test of familiarity is still with us— a proof of quality,—retaining its elegance. I must add, furthermore, that as our first bedstead made its difficult journey up steep and narrow stairs the same genius who had dealt with the settee made a breathless comment. 'You . . . can't,' he said, 'have a better bed than . . . this. The King sleeps . . . in one just . . . like it.'

The King was George the Fifth. Our heads, naturally, lay the more easily for this assurance.

We considered certain other advantages, unconnected with furniture. We already knew that the upper windows commanded a full view of the cricket field and, beyond this, the fine double row of maple trees extending as far as the village itself. We then took pleasure in the fact that the cottage lay well back from the road, protected from too-inquisitive eyes by wide and deep hedges of thorn, holly, and privet, closely involved with each other and, as I found when I came to trim them, vicious to unarmoured hands.

The large front garden was in three sections, containing lawns, a herbacious border, four big rosebeds with edgings of white violas, a small orchard shaded by old apple and plum trees which as we settled in brimmed with blossom, and a vegetable patch where peas and broad beans tempted small birds and gave fine harbourage to many slugs. The hedges were full of busy nests; and the birds occupying them were full of song. A small pond, lively with frogs which are now being driven away from the district by housing and poison-sprays, also contained sticklebacks and what were called soldier-fish, and was (as it still is) a breeding-place for dragonflies of the most iridescent beauty. It can be imagined what these features of country life meant to a pair of untutored urbanites.

Behind the cottage was a very large lawn, decorated with weeping ash trees, and protected from northern winds by a high beech hedge. From certain banks around this lawn peeped the bright eyes of toads; and at dusk we trod carefully because hedgehogs crept mouse-like along the paths. In a rough field at the other side of the beech hedge were trees which by a natural process of multiplication have developed into something of a bird sanctuary; and there pigeons, woodpeckers, magpies, and jackdaws made their nests and their own distinctive contribution to bird noises. Cuckoos arrived from the eighteenth of April; kingfishers paid occasional visits, as did moorhens; owls drifted noiselessly overhead in semi-darkness, squeaking and hooting as they hunted. This, from our point of view, was indeed rural splendour.

Furthermore, as I have said, Lawson Wood had his studio in the garden; and I eagerly appropriated it to my own use. I put all my books, to the number, I suppose, of two or three thousand (they are hard to count) on shelves rising high from the floor; and I established a very large desk which is so highly polished that I have never really liked it. This desk, by the way, looks better in a photograph, where its air of belonging to a business executive is obscured.

The books were not, and are not, treasures for the bibliophile. They were once briefly and truly described by a visiting expert as 'a working library', and they have served me well, not only for work but for instruction and relaxation. If I never bought any more—and with advancing years I have ceased to be, in that respect, self-indulgent—they would serve any man for twenty years of exile in a desert island. Surrounded by them, I am a monarch.

In this studio I can be, and am, as idle as conscience allows, or as industrious as congenital laziness permits. I have worked very hard here; but I have browsed and brooded to my heart's content. So much is evident from the casual distribution of the books and the imperfect tidiness of my highly-polished desk. But I remember with amusement that on his last visit to us Arnold Bennett, that paragon of industry, who had always complained of my lack of application, stood amid the disorder, fixedly contemplating it for several minutes, and at last exploding in a wild cry. The cry was: 'Why haven't *I* got a place like this?'

I could have told him why. The solitude and the atmosphere of leisure (although I have no real leisure), would have bored him to death. He would have wanted to rearrange everything; and bring method into it. He would have counted the number of words he had written that morning, that week, that year, and entered the record in his immense Journal. He would never have idled, never have suffered the haphazard and fitful way in which I turn from one thing to another—now a letter, now some gardening, now a chapter of a manuscript sent to me by a stranger, and now search for some half-remembered passage

41

in this or that author. His motto, like Luther's, was '*Nulla dies sine linea*', which in his case meant 'Never a day without its steady thousand or fifteen hundred words.'

Nor could Bennett have borne to live in rural seclusion. He tried it when he first returned from France to England about 1911, and although attached to Comarques, and even proud of it as an establishment, he was uneasy there. For him the society of other men was a necessity; the engagements of London, its theatres, concerts, its general but hectic activity, were essential stimulants; and, because he slept badly at nights over-full days of work and entertainment provided his best chance of four or five hours of rest in bed.

In these matters I differed from him. My capacity to sleep through the night has been a blessing to one whose nervous energy is exceptional but whose liability to physical exhaustion follows the exercise of that energy. I had experienced the fevered activity of London; and, while nobody enjoys the society of other men and women more than I do, seclusion suits me. I do not recommend the rural life to everybody; some, unquestionably, would despise it as ignoble and unsophisticated. Probably they already despise me for the same defects. I don't care. I have had a happy life.

As a consequence of this temperament, and the corresponding temperament of a wife whose unselfishness and lack of worldly ambition involve no placidity, the whole establishment is in harmony. It is a house in which self-discipline is natural, and where freedom is allowed to others. All guests have sensed this on arrival and during any stay. One, indeed, having suffered restriction and surveillance in stricter homes, where the hostesses watched keenly to prevent any damage being done to carpets and furniture, expressed his enthusiasm in a curious phrase which may call up a false picture of sanded floors and spittoons. He cried vehemently: 'I *like* this place! You feel it doesn't matter where you put your spent matches!'

42

SEVEN

Our Protectors

As we left the railway station on a winter night, finding the temperature several degrees lower than that of London, where we had spent the mid-week, we were greeted by the delicious smell of wood smoke rising from many chimneys. When, carried by a clean but elderly cab, we reached home, it was to find our own logs burning brightly and a hot supper ready. The supper had been prepared, and was brought to table, by a housekeeper who, living not far away, tended the two gifted sons who remained at home (two others were elsewhere, one of them five or six thousand miles away), and shared with us her intimate knowledge of everything that went on in the neighbourhood.

Nobody else had so much information. Her eyes, her ears, her quick mind were alert to catch the smallest event; and her judgment, though never unkind, was immediate. From her we learned all that had happened in our absence, and through her realistic wisdom were enabled to see the villagers, of whatever class, as individuals with histories and characteristics going back for at least three generations.

Our friend was at once a translator and a yardstick, full of humour and perception of human oddity. Her interest in ourselves and others was inexhaustible; and she was superlatively kind. Despite all other activities, she found time and inclination, as well as devoted loyalty, to cook, house-clean, wash, iron, and do all the shopping, while overseeing our domestic lives as a mother might have done.

It could be said, indeed, that she adopted us. We found that she regarded my wife as a clever child, a trifle *naïve* but willing to learn; and myself, though liable to be bamboozled by the unscrupulous, as a model for her sons to copy. She was small, plump, and sturdy, with a mouth rendered small by loss of teeth, and a round, shrewd face. And she was a pearl.

She had first gone out to work for a shilling a week when she was ten, and for more than sixty years had been used to incessant labour. Long a widow, she was never idle and never flustered. At odd times in the evenings, or on Sundays, when she was supposed to be free, she would make special journeys to bring us little treats such as cakes and tarts baked in her own oven, or plants which she thought we should like to grow for ourselves.

There was no limit to her dry merriment over village eccentrics, of whom she had delightful stories. Of some silly or feckless woman she would say, briefly, 'hasn't got all her buttons'; on topers and idlers her comments were withering; of a grand new mincer which I had bought she said nothing to myself but calmly remarked to my wife 'I should think they give him something second-hand.'

Long after a haemorrhage had forced her to give up working for us she remained our close friend. It was she who appointed her successor, who stayed for twenty years and although heard only once to laugh outright was conscientious to the bone. Our thoughts of the successor, also now dead, are warm and cordial; those of our first friend are of deep affection and admiring gratitude.

Nor was she our only support. Lawson Wood bequeathed to us his gardener. This was the most valuable gift he could make to neophytes; for the gardener was a real gardener, who had learned his craft on the estate of the Baron de Worms. There he was under the tuition of a master named Gemmett, whom he often quoted with deep respect as one who had known all things and insisted upon a high degree of care and accuracy in garden and greenhouse.

Our treasure had served in Salonika during the War of 1914–18. He had there been put in charge of Greek labourers, and had performed his duties to admiration. A Hertfordshire man by birth, he had known extreme poverty in boyhood; and apart from impatience with cricketers, whom he suspected of stamping for effect as they slowed down after racing for a ball, he had no animosities. His tenderness to fieldmice, hedgehogs, and stray cats was exemplary.

During his military service, the gardener one day picked up in the camp a discarded copy of the *Iliad* in an English translation. He read it all through; 'it was very interesting.' Though not a great reader (he had too much to do for us and at home) he was garden-learned; and his learning was respected by other gardeners, who would sometimes pay us a visit to get his advice on their problems. He always willingly gave it; and, as is the way with gardeners, sometimes exchanged plants with them for our benefit.

His schemes for our pleasure, constant as they were, held no self-interest. He was absolutely free from that trait. He had to ride a bicycle from his home seven miles away; yet he was always in the house by half-past eight on every weekday. And as he rode he would notice by the roadside small screws, nails and nuts dropped from passing vehicles, which he always picked up and brought to add to a wonderful hoard of such things. What was more, he remembered everything in this hoard, and could produce it at need to solve problems of carpentry or metal-work. We laughed at the hoard; but not to his face.

45

He walked briskly, sometimes singing in a growly voice, and wheeling his tool-laden barrow as if he were going for a picnic. Having heard of gardeners who resented the theft by their mistresses of flowers and partially ripe fruit (Marguerite Bennett complained to me that Arnold's gardener looked at her 'like an *assassin*'), I asked whether he would mind if my wife sometimes picked his flowers. His reply was: 'The garden is yours, sir; and if Mrs Swinnerton likes to pick anything she's welcome to do it.'

He himself picked lavishly on our behalf, bringing in great baskets of raspberries and strawberries in their seasons, and a wealth of vegetables at all seasons. And, finding that he seemed to have no sense of the right time to go home (we heard the tools rattling on his barrow long after dark), I gave him a watch. That made no difference. He continued to work as late as ever, and during the whole of Saturday afternoon, when he should not have been there at all.

Though never personally a clock-watcher, I became uneasy; and asked if his watch had broken. He replied that the watch were a very good watch. I explained my uneasiness. He listened with what I feared was a rather derisive smile, and stood silent. At last he blurted out: 'I . . . er . . . sort of like you, and . . . er . . . sort of get on all right with you. So I . . . er . . . don't bother about the time.'

He did not bother about the time. In the course of our association I gave him two other watches (he lost the first one down our deep well, which was never put to any domestic use); and none of them made the smallest difference to his habits. I shall speak later of the man and his ways.

Pursuing our belief that a home should be a home, we gradually introduced such comforts as seemed desirable. One of these was central heating in six of the rooms (although we still burned logs in high winter), together with electric lighting and power points for electric fires and the vacuum cleaner. At the same time we installed an electrically-operated refrigerator,

46

a new gas cooking-stove, and new geysers in bathroom and scullery for heating water in Summer.

The architect who superintended the central heating also designed a very handsome brick garage, garden shed, and wood shed, with a storage loft covering all three. It is amusing to recall that the estimate for this building was two hundred and fifty pounds, and that the actual bill, when presented, was for several pounds under the estimate.

By degrees we succumbed to Radio, the telephone (chiefly for use by the youngest member of the family), and finally, though with reluctance, to a Television set. These things are known as 'the resources of civilisation'. I name them otherwise; but at least nobody can say that what was built in the days of Queen Elizabeth the First has proved incapable of adaptation to the days of Queen Elizabeth the Second.

Such details may appear smug. They are not smugly related; but are meant to show that residence in a village does not involve total break with the outer world. We still had London at command, and were able to leave home for months at a time to travel on the Continent and in the United States. Looking back, it seems to me that those modest variations of routine, which provided memories for a lifetime, have helped us to value what is not retirement (for we both now work harder than ever), and not acquiescience in comparative obscurity, but what ancient hedonists extolled as quietude of spirit.

EIGHT

Flash-back

I SHOULD LIKE, if I may, to interpolate here an explanation of the fortune by which I was enabled to indulge my dream. It can be skipped by those who are not interested.

These, then, are the heads of a series of events that came in after years to suggest a natural, almost inevitable, pattern. All old men, looking back over their lives, echo Browning's *Sordello* in saying:

> Truth's self, like yonder slow moon to complete
> Heaven, rose again, and, naked at his feet,
> Lighted his old life's every shift and change,
> Effort with counter-effort; nor the range
> Of each looked wrong except wherein it checked
> Some other . . .
> The real way seemed made up of all the ways—
> Mood after mood of the one mind in him.

This is one of the recompenses of age, in days when horizons narrow and rewards must be found in acceptance rather than defiance of rule. One is not dead; the grand expectation that tomorrow will bring some marvellous triumph has merely given place to lively appreciation of benefits received and hopes fulfilled; and contentment, which is so much despised by youth, is seen as a supreme good. An old friend of mine, A. G. Gardiner, as he approached the age of eighty, was in the habit of saying 'Life is adjustment.' Browning, a young man when he wrote *Sordello*, was saying the same thing in verse.

So, as I say, a pattern of events, events created by the contact of character with seized or lost opportunity, forms in memory. My pattern is as follows:

At the age of sixteen I passed from early adventures in editorial affairs to the trade of book publishing. Through the help of my lifelong friend Garfield Howe, whose ambition it was to be a publisher, I became reception clerk in the big show-room of J. M. Dent & Co., then famous for their pocket Temple Shakespeare and Temple Classics. My job was to deal with all visitors, including authors either famous or obscure, artists, printers, stationers, cadgers, and a few sometimes pedantic book-buyers who insisted upon examining perhaps a dozen copies of a book before accepting one of them as exemplary. I had to be courteous, firm, and resourceful; it was a wonderful cure for juvenile self-consciousness, and a wonderful training in the intuitive perception of character.

Unfortunately, some may think, experience in publishing destroyed my awe of authors as a class. Seen in reverse, as it were, authors reveal themselves as vain and desperately sensitive creatures, extraordinarily concerned with publicity, status, reviews, and even sales. This is true of the loftiest of them (I do not mean the greatest, but those who assume superiority to mankind's grosser needs); and my view of them, which though not cruel was less compassionate than it is today, made me incapable of self-importance when I became a writer on my own account.

Indeed, I rarely think of myself as a writer. I do, at times, after reading a short piece, ejaculate 'Not bad', meaning that the piece has a beginning, a middle, and an end; but I never compare myself with other writers when reading their work, and only very recently have I caught myself thinking of some old book of my own as, in retrospect, rather amusing. It is fifty years since I subscribed to a newspaper cutting agency; I see only occasional notices of books I have written, and have the impression (quite inaccurate, I find) that these are invariably unenthusiastic; and was delighted, the other day, at hearing that somebody had said of me: 'Oh, he's not interested in writers; he's more than half a publisher.'

This last may be true.

Even as a boy I was conscious of dual standards—those of judgment and humanity;—and while much more exacting then than I am now, when my tolerance causes the socially or intellectually proud to snort a little, I preferred the humble in spirit. These, while waiting for their interviews, would walk about and come to the window of the little sentry-box in which I stood or sat, talking about themselves or the subjects they were to discuss, asking what I did, and commenting on their former experiences. I thus heard many small details of past and present publishing; reminiscences of the celebrated dead; and current gossip of the living.

I talked—always anonymously—as 'the boy in the box', with Gilbert Chesterton, Hilaire Belloc, and H. G. Wells; and was able to observe the deportment of such different men as W. H. Hudson, Arthur Symons, and Austin Dobson, all of whom, although courteous, attempted no conversation. They sat down, Dobson in a chair, the others on the edge of a long table, in abstracted silence, Hudson so motionless that his skill as an observer of birds and animals became completely intelligible.

It was, however, the artists who proved most friendly of all. They were a jovial crowd, from Herbert Railton, who always addressed me affectionately as 'Johnny', and who drew better when the natural trembling of his hand had been counteracted by slight drunkenness, to the brothers Robinson, whom we knew as Tom, Will, and Charles.

These three swung into the Dent office, full of high spirits, like the Three Musketeers, and J. M. Dent never made any difficulty at all in granting them an interview. As I had to placate and send away so many people whom he did not wish to see, this ready welcome caused me considerable amusement; and one day, when the old man's response to my telephoned inquiry was particularly eager, Charles, bringing up the rear of the mounting trio, looked back and caught me grinning. He raised a jovial finger, and demanded: 'What are *you* laughing at?' I had no need to reply. When they came rattling down the stairs again, all three were laughing. Charles detached himself— he was always the jauntiest of the three—and thrust his head into my box. It was to report Dent's final words. They were truly paternal. 'I'm *proud* of you three boys!' Hence the merriment which justified my grin.

That must have been in 1904. After leaving Dent's in 1907, I saw the Robinsons no more. Tom died; Charles died; Will became 'W. Heath Robinson' and achieved great fame for his complex designs of impracticable machinery; and I, during an illness, grew a beard. Twenty years later, walking in the village, I came face to face with Will. He was unchanged in manner and appearance. He stopped at once, and holding out his hand, he said: 'How are you, Swinnerton?' My reply was: 'I shouldn't have thought you would have known me with this beard.' He retorted: 'I recognised you *behind* your beard.' It transpired that he was a fellow-villager; but his modesty and ultra-respectable demeanour were such that I doubt whether the majority of the villagers ever identified him. He was a most sweet-tempered and attractive man.

I had been taken away from the reception desk and installed in a new post, that of what was called 'confidential clerk' to Hugh Dent, when the head of the firm had an inspiration of genius. Having been very sketchily educated, he was a great lover of books and a great advocate of liberal education for the masses. The two loves had been responsible for his beginnings as a publisher, and especially for the Temple Shakespeare and the Temple Classics. He now determined—this was the inspiration—to create a great new library of a thousand classic volumes, each of which, whatever the number of its pages, was to be produced for one shilling, so that a poor man could own the entire set for fifty pounds.

Setting instantly to work, he planned type-pages and calculated costs to fractions of a farthing. In order to make the books pay, he had to print and sell ten thousand copies of every title, which at the beginning of the century was a very large number indeed. Vehement secret consultations took place for many weeks. Four people alone—Dent himself, his son Hugh, Hugh's 'confidential clerk', and Ernest Rhys, the appointed editor—knew anything of the grandiose scheme. All four kept their mouths shut.

Rhys, a fine-looking, reflective journalist-poet, was the ideal editor for such a series. He had previously conducted two smaller, and excellent series, which showed him to be a sensitive critic, of wide reading; he now showed that he had great patience and superlative tact. Though without genius himself, he could appreciate genius in others, and the long lists of suggestions which he brought daily of books which could rightly claim places in the new series were impressive.

He discussed these lists for hours on end; he bore Dent's irascibility with tolerance; he was sustained, even exalted, by Dent's enthusiasm. And it was he who solved the problem of a striking name for the series. He strode jubilantly into the office one day, crying 'Eureka! *"Everyman's Library"*!'

This was just what Dent wanted—a title to show that the books to be published in a thousand volumes were intended for all; that they were not to be recondite, but fundamentally, while of great range and usually of the highest class, readable. So now began a more general excitement among the staff involved in production. Since Dent was determined that the first fifty volumes should be cast in flood upon booksellers, with a further hundred by the end of the year (1906), its labours became extraordinary. For secrecy's sake a number of different printers were employed; and the results of their work poured into Dent's own bindery. Books were cased at lightning speed. Great bales of them filled every inch of the big basement at Bedford Street. Packing began. For three nights the packers, sleeping on or beside their benches, did not go home at all.

At last, on the appointed day, Everyman's Library was born. The Trade Department was an inferno of shouting booksellers' collectors, with their great sacks, and their extraordinary pronunciations of foreign or classic titles. For ten days two splendid girls typed from nine o'clock in the morning until nine at night letters of my dictation to editors, printers, and booksellers, sometimes apologetic, sometimes minatory, but always with a sense of high purpose. The work was appalling and the monetary rewards to all those devoted workers were negligible; but the triumph of Everyman's Library was complete and glorious, and we all took our share of credit.

In the following year, 1907, I was offered a position as proof-reader with another firm of publishers, Chatto & Windus, where, three years later, I became the reader (in America, 'editor') of all manuscripts submitted to the firm by authors or their agents. Meanwhile, having practised the craft of novel-writing in the evenings and at weekends since I was eighteen, I had my first novel accepted on the very eve of my twenty-fourth birthday. My friends were dubious about the book (friends of young authors are always suspiciously critical; and my own, obsessed by a fear that my natural gaiety might rocket into conceit, were quite insulting); but it was more enthusiastically reviewed than any of them expected, and it sold, as far as I remember, just under 700 copies. At that time this was almost enough to cover the cost of production. I was encouraged to persist.

The second novel was cordially praised by Arnold Bennett, who, I think, may have been attracted to it because Swinnerton is a Staffordshire name; and a newly-established young publisher named Martin Secker suggested that I should write a critical study of George Gissing for a series of what were called 'Modern Monographs'. This study, published in 1912, was a good deal read by literary men; and it was enthusiastically reviewed for a periodical called *Rhythm*, founded by Michael Sadleir, Middleton Murry, and Katherine Mansfield, by Gissing's one-time friend H. G. Wells. This compliment was followed by an invitation to dine at Wells's house in Hampstead.

As I had already met Bennett at lunch, it will be seen that by the time I was twenty-eight, without seeking or even desiring such distinction, I was being almost forcibly befriended by two of the most celebrated writers of the time. Through their kindness the course of my life was changed.

Both insisted upon taking an extraordinarily paternal interest in me from the year 1914, when in a serious illness I lost so much blood and albumen that I nearly died. They asked me to their homes, laughed at my jokes, and in a sense nursed me back to mental energy. At the same time they severely criticised my defects of character. Wells, who gave rein to his emotions, said I was cold by temperament and that my modesty was 'beastly'. Bennett, introducing me to friends, said: 'He is hard. He is crewel. He is also IDLE.' Idleness, in his eyes, was the unpardonable sin. But neither ever lost his temper with me, and both indulged me as an amusing phenomenon.

Between them, they raised a publishers' drudge (but a very happy and fortunate drudge, whose bosses, both Hugh Dent and Percy Spalding of Chatto & Windus, remained close friends to the end of their lives) to a person who became socially familiar with his celebrated elders and enjoyed even some literary standing. By warm praise of a short novel which Martin Secker had asked me to write, they caused this novel, gloomily received in England, where I was told not to do it again, to attract wide attention in the United States, where it sold twenty-five thousand copies.

Such attention had inevitable consequences in England; and as I look back over the years I see this period of my life as rather a glowing one. I was accepted as a novelist of talent; I was considered a good publishers' reader; I had already been invited by the literary Editor of the *Manchester Guardian*, Allan Monkhouse, to contribute reviews to that paper, which had a reputation second to none; and I now became dramatic critic, again by invitations, first to a weekly paper called *Truth*, and then, concurrently, but only on plays of especial interest, to H. W. Massingham's political journal, *The Nation*. What with reading manuscripts from ten to five from Monday to Friday, writing my own manuscripts in off hours, reviewing other men's books from time to time, attending the theatre on several nights a week, writing about what I saw and heard there, and enjoying a good deal of social life in London, I was very active. Too active.

I decided to give up the labours of manuscript-reading and professional attendance at the theatre. Once free of these tasks, I could live where I chose. The country cottage therefore became, not a dream, but a possibility; not only a possibility, but a practical indulgence.

NINE

Walks and Dogs

I HAVE NEVER kept a Journal, as Arnold Bennett did. I wish I could now refer to such a record for details of the events that followed. Or, alternatively, that my memory was as extraordinary as Compton Mackenzie's, which has retained minute impressions gained at every moment of his life. Neither resource is available. My memory has been strong and accurate; but as I have never been much interested in myself it has not been concentrated upon my own affairs.

I know that after spending our honeymoon in Rome my wife and I at first spent only long weekends at the cottage, there entertaining friends who ranged from such American contemporaries as Thomas Beer, who had written studies of Stephen Crane and what he called 'the Mauve Decade', and from school friends of my wife's to those who had long been close to myself—for example, Hugh Dent, Martin Secker, the P. P. Howes, and others, as greatly loved, but unknown to fame. Howe, of course, was the biographer and editor of William Hazlitt, and a friend from boyhood. It was another two years before I could be free enough from London commitments to escape our mid-week residence in a Hampstead flat.

Even then, regular journalistic tasks which included appointments as reviewer or contributor to, successively, *The Evening News*, *The Observer*, and *John o' London's Weekly*, took me to town at least once a week to see editors, so that we did not become completely rural. However, we had much to learn about our garden, which from the first was a great delight; and as the months passed it became clear that one cannot live in a village without becoming a part of it.

The same faces are seen every day, smiles are exchanged, little greetings lead to mutual kindness, and although to this moment I remain anonymous to ladies whose dogs run up for a word of cheer, or to old age pensioners who have 'time to stand and stare', I have a wider and more miscellaneous acquaintance than one would expect in a man whose attention-absorbing business is the writing of books.

To my horror, it has just been pointed out that I have produced fifty-one of these books. The total is appalling; it suggests that I resemble a terrible old man of a former generation who churned out novels at such a rate that long before he reached my present age they had passed a hundred. When it was suggested that something should be done to celebrate the century, a grim Scots journalist replied: 'We might arrange to have it burned by the Common Hangman!' I hope nobody will have this notion about this my fifty-second.

In extenuation of my own pile of perishable goods I can plead only that the first of them was published sixty years ago, and that I have been encouraged to continue both by praise and by moderate popularity. I like people. I like talking about people. Though I have no love of money, I depend for a living on my literary work, which costs me some pains; and while the craft of story-telling is frowned on by those who have no stories to tell it is natural to me to tell stories. In conversation I do this all the time.

Now for a story-teller acquaintance with many people is necessary. It supplies perpetual nourishment to his imagination. Somerset Maugham, who used real models, explained that he did not put whole people into his tales, because they would destroy the proportions of a fictional work. Nevertheless his portraits were recognisable. D. H. Lawrence, who also transferred real people into characters for ferocious exposure, said nothing, but endured some threats of legal proceedings, as well as persecution by offended sufferers. Aldous Huxley satirised members of the intellectual smart set, who were rather flattered by his jovial and non-malignant scorn for their fatuities. I do not draw portraits. I do not consciously observe; I am not, as the satirist is, looking for eccentricity or absurdity to ridicule; I absorb, unawares, by sympathy, and have an immense fund of generalised reference to support invention. If once I lost this capacity for sympathy with ordinary men and women I should grow old and die.

As it is, I can quote the words of a village Police Inspector with whom I was chatting in the High Street. Our colloquy was often interrupted by the need to acknowledge the salutes of passers-by; and as we parted he remarked: 'You and I, between us, must know everybody in this village.'

It happened that for the first six years of residence in the village we were blessed with abnormally fine weather; and as I could concentrate on work during the mornings and long evenings we spent every afternoon in walking about the district. Both were stout walkers. Hills, lanes, main roads (in those days little traffic-laden) were all one to us. Probably our walks were not more than about ten miles in any direction; but they were all good, and some were better than others. The old solicitor whom I mentioned on page 19, with whom I struck up acquaintance, had as his hobby the defence of footpath rights. He helped with advice. And the best walk of all took us to the top of a bracken-covered hill from which we could survey one of the most beautiful stretches of country in Southern England, with the South Downs forming a serene background. This was the beauty which makes Englishmen love their land unawed and without extravagant sentiment.

On these walks we saw nightingales singing by daylight; yellowhammers, which shun dwellings; and pheasants, not at all frightened, running across the lanes a few yards ahead. Amid the verdant panorama red-tiled roofs stood like little islands. And once, from the hilltop, we followed the course of swiftly moving black clouds which reminded us of a Constable picture until, without warning, a deluge caused us to run down the hill and take refuge under the roof of an inn where smugglers were known to have brought their brandies in the eighteenth century. Under the hill was an old cottage in the garden of which the owner collected the broken fragments of small clay pipes used by soldiers at the time of the Peninsular War. All these experiences, to us, were great adventures.

One curious thing was that very often a dog—always a different dog—would appear, give us a sharp glance, and decide to join the ramble. This is a habit of dogs, which, like other animals, and even chickens, show great fondness for human company. They do not adopt a proprietorial air, but roam at will, sniff agreeable smells, leave their own messages for fellow-dogs, and at last, without farewell, step away to their homes for tea. They have been in touch for several miles, enjoying the walk and the company.

This is not a habit peculiar to English dogs. Once, when we were staying at a small resort on the Mediterranean coast, we were adopted in the same way by two French mongrels. These accompanied us on a number of occasions; one of which, in particular, produced a curious incident. We were going up a hill, when the dogs, which had previously been roving in all directions, and sometimes disappearing altogether, came very close to us, showing signs of anxiety, and kept alongside with tails down and stomachs near the ground. We were mystified by the change, until we reached the gateway of a large house standing back from the road. Beside the gateway was a notice, which said: CHIEN MÉCHANT.

Although our companions were French, I do not suppose

that they could read. Therefore instinct, or previous experience, must have warned them of danger. As soon as we had safely passed the gate they gambolled as before, scampered ahead, and were presently lost to sight. We did not take that road again when they were in attendance.

No *chien méchant* seemed to live near our village. Nor, although I have noticed concern on the part of female dog-owners at sight of some larger animal at a distance, have I noticed what Mr Polly's friend called a fracass between them. But the village is full of dogs, many of which sit majestically in stationary cars, sometimes three or four at a time, while others perch beside the drivers of vans. Those on foot run, on or off their leads, on the Common. Others again roam quite by themselves; and two elderly dogs, unconnected, and without visible owners, take appalling risks by walking sedately across the roads in front of oncoming cars as if they cared nothing for such impertinences. Occasionally one of these wanderers will take a dislike to a particular vehicle and, throwing off the thoughtfulness of age, will fly after it, barking very loudly indeed.

Small parties of unescorted friends meet with much tail-wagging. They jostle and pummel each other for ten minutes or so, and then lie down with open mouths, panting, well content with their previous diversion. In the end they part, with further tail-wagging, having agreed, it seems, to meet again on the morrow. Two regularly chase a ball in the early morning, sometimes before it is light. The ball, we know, is thrown by their mistress, whom they unquestionably obey when the time comes to re-cross the main road on their way back to breakfast.

These are but a few of the many dogs living in our village. Indeed, I have never seen so many dogs before, even at Brighton, where they bark at the waves and sometimes splash in pursuit of sticks. They range from Borzois and Dalmatians to Pekinese and Corgis, with perhaps a slight preponderance of Labradors. The Corgis are fat and slow and friendly; the

Labradors seem to be preoccupied with their own affairs. One of the latter sits outside our butcher's shop every morning, a model of patience. When I tell the butcher that he must be very hard-hearted not to respond by rushing out with a bone my reproach is met with calm irony; but obviously no dog would keep such daily vigil without reason. This one looks very well fed. I believe the butcher is his friend.

TEN

Remarkable Visitors

W E SOON found that cats, as well as dogs, lived a different kind of life in the country. Although attached to their homes by day, they rove by night at all seasons of the year, especially when called by instinct to a corroboree around a female of the species. At such times they will desert their homes for several days, only running in for a hasty snack at long intervals.

Not only home-bred cats do such things. Others, living one does not know where, turn up irregularly for meals. There must be some system among them, as there is among tramps, which amounts to a signposting of promising routes: 'Good eats at the Pines,' or 'The Laurels.' This must be so, for in the course of rural existence we have been waited on by cats of all breeds and sizes. They have ranged from deserted mothers with kittens in their mouths or at their heels to combative creatures ready to fight to the death any other cat crossing their path.

A number of these have caused us trouble. One, in particular, was completely wild. He was jet black, with bright green eyes; and gave the impression that somewhere in his ancestry there was a strain of Siamese. Although savage, he was demonstratively affectionate, lurching against our legs with such strength that we tottered; and his purr was like the roaring engine of a stationary tractor. We developed a rather apprehensive regard for him. Unfortunately, gratitude for kindness received affected him so strongly that he often pounced upon his benefactors. Protected by trousers of substance, I could afford to smile, but my wife was less well-armoured. Her leg was seized and clawed with such enthusiasm that she had to be taken, torn and bloody, to the village hospital for treatment.

Much against our will, we were forced to summon the Local Inspector of the R.S.P.C.A. He, full of admiration for a splendid animal, took our friend away, hoping to be able to tame him. Alas, that proved impossible; and poor Impo, as we called him, was thereafter painlessly destroyed.

All other visitors have been more gentle, though none more affectionate. No foxes, and only one rabbit, hideous with myxomatosis, ever joined us. Several flights of peewits have descended for a while; moorhens have reared their long-legged families, which ran about the lawn as if quite tame; innumerable butterflies, from Tortoiseshells and Red Admirals to the lovely Painted Ladies, were once common sights among the vegetables. They no longer come, probably because the whole butterfly population has diminished in this part of the world. And one day in 1964 a sensational event occurred which we shall never forget.

In that Summer a long row of African Marigolds grew in a bed beside the path to our side gate. This row was in full bloom, a mass of rather deeper than orange-coloured flowers, handsome to behold. I was walking down the path when my eye was caught by the swift fluttering of two very large and astonishingly beautiful butterflies. To my eyes they were a glowing black, with broad orange or golden bands and a profusion of white spots at the outer edges of the wings. I had never before seen such butterflies.

63

Deeply impressed, I called my wife; and we watched the pair with deep excitement. So excited were we that I ran indoors for pencil and paper, made a rough sketch, and noted the colours for later elaboration. The butterflies departed; but we had our record, which we preserved. Some time afterwards I was lunching with the trusty Compton Mackenzie (whom I have now known for nearly sixty years); and, remembering that he is expert in butterflies, as he is in wild flowers, Manx cats, and so many other things, I took my coloured sketch with me.

When consulted, Mackenzie produced his little magnifying glass and scrutinised the drawing. Then he stirred with excitement comparable to my own, saying: 'I'm almost sure they were Camberwell Beauties. Let me have this sketch, and I'll send it to John Campbell, who knows more about butterflies than anybody else.'

Sure enough, John Campbell subsequently wrote from the Isle of Canna, where he lives, confirming Mackenzie's identification; and his word was super-confirmed by S. N. A. Jacobs, editor of *The Entomologist's Record*. Jacobs pointed out a slight inaccuracy in my order of colour; but had no doubt at all of the fact. Camberwell Beauties are rare emigrants from Scandinavia; and while those we saw *may* have been bred artificially in England it was unquestionable that we had been astoundingly fortunate. I still have my drawing, and a coloured print sent to me for comparison by Mr Jacobs; and the two, with accompanying correspondence, prove that once upon a time we did really entertain angels unawares.

PART TWO
Life at the Cottage

ONE

Disturbance

IT MAY be thought that I have written so far in the vein of Pangloss, in *Candide*, who thought that everything was for the best in this best of all possible worlds. I remind the impatient that for the most part I have been describing what happened in the early and middle nineteen-twenties. The First World War had been over for long enough to allow illusions of peace to creep back into normal minds. I had just returned to England after travelling all through the United States, where I had made many new friends, and where I was regarded as at least a representative novelist of the younger generation. And I appreciated my luck. The picture I have given of this luck and its accompaniments has been a true one.

I do not think this is the best of all possible worlds. It has greatly changed since I was born towards the end of the much-condemned Victorian age, in some respects for the better, but not always, I think, for the greater happiness of its inhabitants. When I was very young food was cheap and plentiful; there was much unemployment, so that loss of a job was dreaded as leading possibly to starvation and death; and often a week's notice could make all the difference between the possession of a home and the gradual dispersal of every one of its treasures.

As the twentieth century began, Britain was engaged in a war in South Africa which, although the settlement following it did her credit, diminished the national grandeur and saw the end of confident Imperialism. There was still vast wealth at home and overseas; but liberal-minded people had been greatly troubled by the war, and the failure of British generals to adapt their strategies to an enemy who would not observe the textbook rules had been humiliating to those who were called Jingoes ('We don't want to fight; but by Jingo if we do'). There was accordingly a stir of humanitarian resolve; and poor people began, not to count their blessings, as they had done for centuries, but to raise their voices and demand attention.

When many people raise their voices the din is considerable. The Liberal Governments of 1906 and 1910 gave much time to social legislation; the Conservatives thought protective tariffs would help our own workers at the expense of workers in other countries; and other countries prepared to conquer the markets of the world at the expense of the British. We heard a cry from the Germans for 'living room'; and were warned by the German Kaiser of 'the yellow peril'.

Two wars have followed which killed, maimed, and terrorised millions of people. Between and after these wars we have seen revolutions abroad, government at home by increasingly official authority, the Welfare State, the Permissive Society. The cry of 'Fair Shares for All', once a slogan, has given way to 'A Bigger Slice of the Cake' and bands of vocal millionaires. There has been an uprising of violence everywhere; and a Cambridge professor, apparently unaware that another Cambridge professor, Bertrand Russell, said much the same thing many years ago, has delivered a Radio message acclaiming the imminence of moral chaos and total destruction of the family as a unit of society.

I shall not now discuss Cambridge professors and their conceptions of a brave new world. I only mention them in order to show that our village, which has heard of such things, contains many other folk who resent every arbitrary interference with their tranquillity. The First World War, which caused the loss of many young lives here as elsewhere, seemed in 1923 to have made comparatively little difference to the community as a whole.

The Second World War was a different matter. During the first year of it, which in Southern England was a year of brilliant sunshine, we slept largely undisturbed by the threat of personal danger. When France collapsed we became, owing to the nearness of the Channel coast, immediately vulnerable. Canadian troops, tough and highly-trained, were drafted into the district as part of the first line of defence. One saw them everywhere. The lads of the village, after watching the sport of baseball, became for a time baseball fans; the more circumspect among our dazzled girls now live overseas. The troops are still held in great respect; and a few of them revisit us as elderly travellers, claiming to have introduced some of their own maples into the Common's noble chain.

Our young men went to fight abroad, some in France, others in Burma, Italy, and North Africa, or—a popular service in a countryside within range of Portsmouth—in the ships of the Royal Navy. At first only these presences and absences reminded us of the nearness of war. On certain days a dull thudding in the far distance would be associated with heavy artillery or anti-aircraft fire. Observation posts were manned in case German planes should fly inland. Otherwise, except at night, when blinds were drawn and wardens were alert, we might have imagined ourselves in the peaceful village we first knew.

At last the German planes did come, not in fleets, but as single raiders. One of them bombed a stationary train in which sat local schoolgirls on their way home. Others, at night, were at least heard overhead, and when one or two were brought down near at hand it became clear that danger was very near indeed.

Airfields seemed to sprout all about us. Every evening a curious monster that we named 'the Crystal Palace' (it was really, I believe, a movable beacon for the guidance of British airmen) trundled past the cottage on its way to a commanding hill, to trundle home again to some unknown lair in the early morning. Subsequently the flying bombs, heralded by Goebbels's promise that they would raze the homes of Surrey plutocrats, rattled overhead and exploded to the general alarm. There were many such bombs. Whether they were aimed at the village or the airfields, or whether they had been diverted from their original course, I cannot say. They were not as constant with us as they were in South London, where a Brixton woman remarked to my sister-in-law, a fellow-resident: 'I don't *like* these flying bombs, do you? I don't *mind* them; but I don't *like* them.'

One, however, arriving in the early morning, skimmed our roof and crashed in a field just beyond the garden, cracking the cottage walls and bringing down some ancient plaster. Another, on an afternoon when, after I had been to London, we were having tea by the open windows, was swallowed by a gas-container on the other side of the main road, killing a woman who had come to her back door at the sound of the warning 'alert', and in the vagaries of its blast breaking many shop windows at a greater distance while leaving our own home untouched.

And, warfare becoming ever more closely concentrated as between Germany and Britain, we often heard a long, low, steady roar, and in the fading daylight saw what looked like an extraordinary flock of migrating birds. They flew very high; tiny specks covering the sky from end to end of vision; and they were British bombers on their way to Germany. When the return journey was made round about dawn we found among the flower-beds mysterious scattered strips of silver paper. At first these were very puzzling; afterwards they proved to be discarded remnants of a device used to distract the radar of German defenders. We kept some of them, and some scraps of the flying bombs, until the War was over, when they were better forgotten.

One vivid memory of these War years is of a night when the activity of mobile guns showed that enemy planes were overhead. I stood outside the door of a bedroom in which a very little girl lay asleep. If I decided that the danger was too acute for any further risk to be taken I was hastily to wrap the child in a blanket and carry her downstairs; and as I waited I could see my wife standing below in the half-light, with, pressed close to her skirt, an ever-present small black-and-white cat, who could not bear to be parted from us in these moments of suspense.

No bomb was dropped. The guns passed. The little girl slept on. We heard at length the long-drawn 'All Clear'; and as I crept downstairs again the small cat, her fears relieved, skidded round a door and peeped back at us to show her eagerness for yet one more game of hide and seek. Her jubilance at the passing of anxiety was so comic that we burst out laughing.

Not every memory is as happy as that. One curious and saddening incident occurred during the plague of flying bombs. As was widely noticed at the time, the blast caused by these discreditable engines travelled incalculably, so that in one case windows near at hand were shattered, while in another the danger occurred at a tangent, often far away. On a summer afternoon, when there had been no alert, we were astonished by the sudden slamming of every door in the cottage, followed by complete silence. A bomb had fallen three miles away. Only afterwards did we find that the explosion which had caused our doors to slam had blown a nest from the honeysuckle growing over and beside the porch. It was that of regular visitors, a pair of spotted flycatchers. Beside the broken nest lay the bodies of five fledglings; and the parents had disappeared. Flycatchers have never again nested in the honeysuckle; nor, indeed, in the garden.

TWO

A Word for Spiders

THE WAR passed; and so have another twenty years in which many changes have occurred in our lives; but a constant interest remains. This is the watching of birds in the garden. Those little brown flycatchers, with their notably high, intelligent brows and lovely darting flashes from one vantage point to another, perhaps began our observations, which are a little better informed than they once were.

The observations still have no scientific value. We lack the time and patience to emulate a devoted band which is contributing to international understanding by the exchange of systematically-kept records of migration habits, and in many cases protection of nesting grounds. To hear members of the band speak over the air with enthusiasm of their craft is to be greatly stimulated; for such men have no hesitation in sharing their knowledge with both other experts and such members of the laity as ourselves. Their aim is common understanding.

We, as beginners, first had to identify the birds living in the garden. We saw them at work in a herbaceous border and on the rosebeds. We were familiar, of course, with London sparrows, the pigeons and pelicans in St James's Park, the astonishing clusters of starlings at night and in the mornings on domes and ledges near Whitehall and St. Martin-in-the-Fields, where they look like swarms of bees; but other varieties were novel, and their songs had been unheard. We gradually learned to recognise the birds, their songs, their seasons.

We learned, for example, that goldfinches arrived in numbers when the nettles beyond the garden were in bloom, that bull-finches and hawfinches visited when they could raid the peas, and that apples were pecked before they were ripe by black-birds. We began to spot tree-creepers on our pile of logs, and siskins and whitethroats at their first coming. We learned which birds were the gardener's friends and which his enemies, as much from their behaviour to ourselves as to the condemnations or praises of the gardener himself. And, month by month, we saw martins nest in the woodshed, swallows assemble on the telegraph wires, and the cuckoo rest awhile on our ash trees to prove that he was more than a 'wandering voice'. It was all, for us, an innocent pastime; and as I am greatly in favour of innocent pastimes, such as cricket and bird-watching, the pleasure we took in the occupation was unsullied.

Just why flying creatures should charm, while those running on and into the earth are considered to be vermin, I do not understand. Nor why these latter should be viewed by women with fear or disgust. No doubt brilliant plumage is magnetic; but not all birds are brilliant, and the difference in colouring between a wren and a fieldmouse is inconsiderable. If anything, the advantage is with the mouse, that shy and tender little being which, if discovered in the house, hides its face in a corner, hoping thereby to make itself invisible. It, and the tiny sharp-nosed shrew, vie in pathetic harmlessness.

I believe there must lie in the aversion felt for mice by women an old dread dating from the period of long skirts, when a fugitive seeking cover could cause panic. Now that skirts are short, and women bold to the point of nakedness, such panic cannot arise. Nor have I noticed any shuddering in the younger generation, which in this respect as in many others (for instance the driving of small cars in vehement traffic) shows a steadiness of nerve possessed only by exceptional women in the Victorian era. Hamsters are quite as well-loved by small girls as by small boys. Even snakes are fearlessly seen and handled by the young of both sexes. I hope, therefore, that the hysteria produced in one old woman, now dead, but at the time living two doors away, by an innocent hedgehog seen in the dusk is a thing of the past.

Alas, spiders are still too often a cause of disgust and fear. Their webs are ruthlessly destroyed by the whisk of a brush, a habit on the part of housewives which throws us back to bad old days when books were forbidden in the home as harbourers of dust. It is true that books sometimes get a little dusty. It is also true that spiders are book-lovers. I cannot take out a volume of my big thirteen-volume *Oxford Dictionary* without disturbing them and finding their discarded coats in the rough edges of every page. But they have not damaged the pages, as detestable silverfish do; and books in more constant use are unaffected.

Books are now, in civilised homes, considered decorative. Their bright covers and gold letterings, which catch the sun and the firelight, radiate warmth. They are sometimes taken from the shelves for perusal; but when unread they live on. I wish that in time spiders may enjoy the comparable esteem to which they are entitled.

They are models of intelligence, patience, and helpfulness— as Bruce long ago discovered. The smaller ones launch themselves into space as boldly as parachutists. Like poets and novelists, those of all sizes create from within themselves all the material needed for their craft, and in addition spin their own homes and are their own providers. Bird-lovers may complain that they do not sing; but this could be because their voices are pitched too high for the human ear to register.

If they sing, I think their songs must resemble the cackling of the witch in *Hansel and Gretel*. She is obviously the prototype of all spiders. Their humour, as well as their art and determination in spinning alternatives to the webs destroyed by those cruel brushes, links them with authors whose books are just as callously attacked by reviewers of no creative skill. It should be granted and admired. It is to be read in gleaming eyes and eager movements. For their victims, which are among the few things I detest, I have no sympathy. Their only value is as food for spiders.

Spiders are also masters (or mistresses) of the fundaments of architecture. They know where best to build their webs, near windows, or in corners, or across air-paths used by flies, and how to protect them from the stresses of wind and weather. I can give one instance of this from my own observation. My studio (once Lawson Wood's) has an overhanging porch or hood, supported by angled struts, but open to the wind. On a sunny day this porch is an ideal place for flies, sated with unholy and unhygienic feasts, to bask and sleep off the effects of repletion. Spiders, knowing this, arrive in good time, and spin from hood to strut with long threads which keep their webs in place.

One Summer day, however, a wind arose. The resident spider found his web being violently shaken, and threatened with destruction. His threads, being attached only from above, were inadequate. Obviously something had to be done to create a true balance; but the ground was at least four feet below, and although he could spin a thread of that length the result could not be satisfactory. What could he do? By some extraordinary legerdemain he obtained a tiny stone, the weight of which would supply just the stability he needed. He made a noose about the stone.

It was at this point I observed him. There hung the thread, with the stone, round, flat, and the size of sixpence, in place and effective. The spider himself had already shinned up his cable to an undisturbed corner. I could hardly believe my eyes;

75

but when I summoned witnesses they, although at first incredulous, could do nothing but confirm the fact. The spider, watching our investigations, showed the indulgent calm of genius.

I have never known such a thing to happen again. That one instance, however, was enough to produce respect, even awe, in my estimate of spiders as reasoning creatures. Wasps, too, unlike bees (which allow themselves, as horses do, to be exploited by mankind), are unusually intelligent; but spiders, for me, hold the palm. What a pity that they have no publicity agents to break down lack of appreciation in the home! I sympathise with them in this; for I have no publicity agent to circulate stories of my own subtle performances.

The one folly of spiders seems to be a habit of falling into polished baths or sinks which they cannot clamber out of. Even this apparent lapse may be due to a kind of sportiveness; for when rescued by sponge or dish-mop they remain quiescent until exactly the right moment, and then take a flying leap to safety, scampering off like children released from school. I wish I could hear their answers to my comments and inquiries. To my regret, they emulate Jesting Pilate, and do not stay to answer.

THREE

Our Feathered Friends

I RETURN TO birds, some of which eat spiders.

One question that will always perplex me concerns their names. I do not need to be told that many are derived from tongues other than our own, nor that some, such as peewits and cuckoos, are imitations of the birds' own cries, nor that country names—ousels, throstles, and corbies, for instance—are used in ancient English ballads. I am thinking rather of the fact that while golden orioles, lyre-birds, vultures, hawks, and eagles are distinctive names, and those of woodpeckers and treecreepers represent simple observation of familiar habits, blackbirds, so called, are no blacker than rooks or crows or jackdaws. Why are they merely 'blackbirds'?

Did invention suddenly fail those who first gave names? If so, it is really discreditable to them. In any case, female blackbirds are not really black; they are very little darker, except for the familiar scarlet waistcoats, than robins, and one can detect a faint speckle in their brown breasts. Is jealousy of a finer breast display the reason why they are always so unkind to thrushes? Thrushes have an advantage, also, in grace; but this, surely, does not account for the hostility.

As a learner-gardener, I soon found that, among garden birds, the female blackbird, especially when she has young in the nest, is almost tamer than the robin. Robins, having centuries of good relations with gardeners behind them, attend all digging operations, jumping down fearlessly into a trench, and, if the spade is out of use for a few moments, perching on its handle. This is because they are insect-catchers and are recognised as such by the merest tyro. They are also popular because of their bright eyes, delicate legs, perky movements, and blithe twitter at all seasons of the year. Who can refuse a smile at the sound of that twitter in the dusk, or before the dawn?

The equally courageous blackbirds, however, which come inquisitively to investigate one's activities and seem to say 'What do you think you're doing in my garden?' are known as strawberry-eaters; and it is they who sample the unripe apples. They ought not to be so bold. It is the boldness of impudence; they exult in it. When discovered in the act of theft they pretend alarm, and fly off with ribald squawks which resemble the titters of little vulgar girls, returning a few seconds later as if they had never done anything amiss.

Sentimentalists assert that the birds attack only vermin-infested fruit; and that if a pan of water is laid near the strawberries no fruit will be taken. This suggestion causes experienced gardeners to laugh morosely; for they know that all birds recognise good fruit when they see it, and, being incurably greedy, take it. As George Robey used to sing:

> 'If something should please,
> That something I seize,
> With no "by your leave";
> I just grab it.'

We must beware of sentimentalising the brazen.

That they are brazen, no observer will deny. When nestlings

78

are to be fed they will eat almost anything. For two years we had a mother blackbird close at hand, identifiable at sight by a white feather in one of her wings, and always waiting by the back door at dawn for customary tit-bits. Her attitude of humble expectancy was such that we called her Uriah Micawber, Uriah for short. If the door was left open, as in Summer it often is, she would enter the house, prospecting for the cat's 'overs', and going so far as to attempt intimidation of the cat himself.

The cat made no attempt to molest Uriah. On the contrary, he showed respect for her; and I have often seen the pair, at a distance of no more than two yards, eyeing each other with obvious interest. The cat, being well fed, was in no need of a mouthful of feathers; Uriah, thinking of her babies, was ready to wait, and determined to outstare the enemy for the sake of rewards to come. They always came.

We forgive fruit-thefts by blackbirds because of their beautiful song, which begins before daylight and continues for as long as the sun's afterglow can be seen from any high perch. They are the most constant and vociferous singers in our garden, sitting alone in the upper branches of an apple tree or on the highest ridge of the roof. They sing, as nightingales will do, within a few feet of man, daring him, it seems, to punish their less creditable performances. And they sing like boasters.

Experts claim that they do it to establish territorial rights. I disagree. I think they praise their own achievements as nest-builders, husbands, family-producers and hunters. I think they are like women with washing-machines, refrigerators, and a new drawing-room carpet, or men with new cars or sons who are doing well at school. The claim to territorial rights is a minor affair, shown to wanton rivals on the ground, who try to appropriate individual crumbs or worms. Then there are sudden rushes and scuffles. But in the air, I say, singers at a distance are challenged to repeat their ridiculous pretensions to greater talent. What we hear is joyous brag and self-content.

It is as natural for birds to sing as it is for experts to scribble in their note-books, and far more spontaneous. Some humans (but apparently not the experts) have been known to sing or whistle very lustily in their baths, or when engaged in whittling sticks or some other absorbing task. As a boy I used to whistle a great deal myself, from good spirits, as I walked the streets of London; and even now, when whistling comes less readily, I can make a blackbird cock his head and listen to the opening bars of Waldteufel's *Grenadiers* waltz. He thinks for one instant that I am another blackbird.

I do not want to labour this contradiction of the experts; but I insist that all birds sing when there is no danger of invasion of territorial rights. It is either at the day's beginning or at the day's end, either in hope or in reflective satisfaction. They sing also for and with mild and rainy weather, which promises a harvest of surfacing worms. 'This is good,' they say. 'And everything in the garden is lovely!'

Now while he always rushes violently towards a harmless thrush, who, as airmen used to say, takes evasive action, the blackbird shows one illuminating piece of cowardice. He is always afraid of the rough, long-beaked starling whose bad manners disconcert all other birds who are not conspicuously larger. He will tolerate, without seeming to notice, theft from under his beak of some choice morsel by a cheeky sparrow; but will move quickly away from a starling. Why does he allow the sparrow such liberties? Can it be that he is a little slow in the wits? It is a charge that cannot be brought against any sparrow in England.

FOUR

Songsters

A POINT I should like to make is that as a rule there is quite remarkable tolerance among birds. Starlings will jump in the air as I imagine cocks do in a main, attacking each other with fury; but one never sees a rough and tumble between a tit and a chaffinch, or a robin and a sparrow. The appearance of a magpie will alarm all small birds, as the sight, miles in the air, of a hawk will cause hens to run to cover; yet I have never seen a magpie attack. Very likely his interest is in eggs and nestlings. Magpies live in the field behind our garden. If they fly in the orchard it is always in the early morning, when humans are not about. Nevertheless one sees them on roads at all times of day, and occasionally they do a little prospecting on the back lawn.

They and the jackdaws, who also nest beyond the garden, send emissaries to watch for scraps from the top of a big ash tree; and when scraps are thrown these emissaries summon their brethren with croaks of 'Good! Good!' Both jackdaws and magpies behave as if they feared to be shot, which I think never happens around us, although pigeons, which steal much that farmers value, do occasionally give rise to startling bangs in local fields. This fear is inexplicable to me.

Nor do I understand why larger birds have such harsh voices. When we speak of 'bird song', we really imply the warble produced by nothing bigger than a blackbird. The late Sir Harry Johnston used to keep peacocks at his old priory near Arundel, and I never heard anything uglier than the noise they made. Vultures and eagles are outside my experience; but crows and rooks (and I suppose ravens, as one hears the phrase 'as hoarse as a raven') make sounds which, amusing as they are, cannot be called song. Jackdaws have a petulant call, which reminds me of the cries formerly reached by cultivators of the Lytton Strachey falsetto. Ducks quack; flying geese screech; the cock's morning trump, inspiriting as it is, misses beauty; and the pheasant's call is as rusty as the turning of an old key in an unoiled lock. As for the cuckoo, he is best heard in the background of a dawn chorus or as part of a musical composer's mélange of Summer or woodland impressions. I have no objection to any of these vocal efforts; I say only that, to my ear, they are as tuneful as a frogs' chorus.

Another question over which I find myself puzzling is that of variations in flight. When a skylark is mounting high, he sings, and one can see his wings beating very fast. What he does when he reaches whatever altitude he sets as a goal, I do not know; he is then beyond ordinary sight. Whether the smaller garden birds also use their wings for more than a second is also mystery to me. It is true that their flights are brief, and they volplane very easily; but they seem to flutter hardly at all as they dart into a hedge. Swallows evidently flutter very fast for short distances, and then dive; hawks and owls float on their large, broad wings; and pigeons have a slow, steady beat. But rooks, when they fly singly, seem to make heavy weather of their journeying. Is it because their bodies are heavy, or their wings relatively short? Has it to do with the height at which they fly? Is it only when they are battling against the wind?

Probably the experts know. I do not. In gardens, most birds hop; but from the wagtail upward they seem able to run, and in the case of wagtail and thrush the run is extraordinarily graceful.

When the woodpecker, or yaffle, calls, country people prick their ears and say the short warble is a prophecy of rain. I am not sure that this is really the case; but the yaffle calls seldom, and he may occasionally misread the signs. One hears him tapping on a clear day. He also frequents our lawn, as devoted to his prodding search as are the starlings. He is as brilliant in his green and scarlet plumage as the kingfisher is in his electric blue. Both are aloof birds.

At one time a kingfisher caused havoc among goldfish in our pond. Once he had been detected, we gave the fish a covering of wire-netting; but he adroitly penetrated this, and went off in triumph. Only when the pond had been completely covered was he baffled. One Sunday morning we chanced to look out of a bedroom window overlooking the pond, and saw his performance as he flew from point to point for as long as half-an-hour, trying to beat the obstacle. He was obviously puzzled and annoyed. At length, deciding that no hope remained, he flew off and came no more.

There are now no fish in the pond: all were removed by little boys during one of our absences from home, and we did not replace them. But blackbirds and sparrows use it, bathing or sipping from the shallow water around certain rocks of ragstone. I gather that farmers dislike sparrows. I do not. They will fly down to food a dozen at a time, and if quick to seize scraps they are content to feed *en masse*, often from the same dish, like well-bred guests at a gypsy-party 'dipping their fingers in the stew'. I grant that they mangle the yellow crocuses, and I think also early primroses; but they are extremely helpful over greenfly on the roses, and on balance I imagine they do more good than evil in the garden. One must not say this to professional gardeners; but are professional gardeners, hoarding their peas, any more just than farmers?

Surely hawfinches and bullfinches, if less numerous, are individually more destructive.

Those occasional outbursts of wild twittering which announce a family row among sparrows are not, I think, over food. They appear to be a protest against infringement of some clan taboo. I have never ascertained the cause, and all trouble is as short-lived as its outburst has been sudden. The birds do not sing; they chirp; and the chirp seems to be merely exclamatory. I therefore regard them as virtuous little birds. I would sooner trust a crowd of them with a strawberry bed than a single blackbird, for all the blackbird's pretence that he is only scuffling for insects under the leaves.

The greediest birds in the garden are the tits. One of our neighbours remarked to me a few years ago: 'They always take my first row of peas. So this year I'm dishing them. I'm not *planting* a first row of peas.' I could not help wondering whether the tits would recognise the difference between a first and a second row, or whether they would merely assume that the gardener had been a little dilatory, and eat as before.

During the winter we always hang half-coconuts from an apple tree in sight of the dining-room windows, and consequently see the tiny birds eating all day long. They are lovely to watch; and they assemble in great variety, from the minute blue-and-yellow to the long-tailed and the almost black-backed coal tit. Sometimes twenty or thirty at a time will flutter on to the hanging nuts and bags and cases of peanuts, savagely pecking, and being dislodged only by the arrival of other impatient diners. These flutter their wings to arouse alarm and create opportunity for themselves; and the same tactics are repeated and imitated, until the air is filled with flying rivals. In hard times the demolition of nuts is so rapid that I almost tire of bringing home peanuts and sawing coconuts. While replenishing the store I am watched from the surrounding hedge by many bright eyes; and as soon as my back is turned the feast is resumed. Other birds rest; the tits never do so.

84

Last winter they were joined and justled by strangers who are more obviously aggressive. These are two pairs of greenfinches and at least one pair of nuthatches, whose longer beaks enable them to raid with instant effect. They do not stay long; but they return, always with hostility to the native tits. The greenfinches are Summer residents, whose very sweet song is delightful to hear. The nuthatches come only occasionally. But in the past two years there have been other strangers, larger and more gymnastic, who gnaw ferociously at the good things provided for all. They are a greater menace to the garden than any birds, even bullfinches, even pigeons could be. They are two grey squirrels.

These squirrels first arrived because, while prospecting, they found hazel nut trees growing in the outskirts of the orchard and in one of our hedges. Believing themselves to be in the land of plenty, they raided the nut-trees, and tried to bury their treasures in lawns and rose-beds. So profuse was the crop that we found nuts scattered everywhere, uneaten, and still in their husks. This was prodigality. It was followed, as the growing season passed, by unprincipled digging in all parts of the garden. Evidently squirrels, like old men, forget. They forget where their treasure lies; and, having forgotten, they first prospect wildly and then rob everybody else.

Their size, rather than any assault, frightens away the tits. The squirrels, having the feast before their eyes, slip along a branch, and, clinging to it with adhesive hind feet, reach at full length down the hanging strings, haul them up, clasping the nut to their bosoms. When strength fails, they try to carry the prize off to their dreys, and after biting through the string, so that the nut drops to earth, they are seen to grip its edge with sharp teeth, support it with forepaws, and stagger along, erect, like a human being with too heavy a burden.

Not having been built to walk so, they are constantly baffled, with evident chagrin. By some device or other they do coax the food for some distance; and we have several times recovered a coconut, abandoned, half the garden away. Only by a system of wiring the nuts, either to the tree or to rose bushes, have we been able to protect the tits from what would otherwise be wholesale banditry.

I am here reminded of another instance of ingenuity, and a duel between our gardener and a rat. This rat appreciated the fact that apples were stored in a loft above the garage and sheds. It proceeded to feed lustily, carrying off whole apples and leaving others half-nibbled on the floor of the loft. Steps had obviously to be taken to check the thief; and all possible entrances were plugged. The plugging did not avail; apples continued to disappear or remain nibbled.

At last, in his search for the enemy, B., the gardener, discovered a large box in which two rooms had been contrived, one for sleep, the other as a store where the missing apples were kept. Both rooms were clean and tidy. This was no ordinary rat. Appreciating his quality, but wishing to keep his own store, B. set a trap. It was ignored. That, naturally, was a challenge. Against his inclination, but feeling that this must now be a fight to a finish, B. invested in some infallible white tablets, and laid one of them temptingly near the rat's house.

Next day he came indoors dancing with glee, and crying: 'He's ate the tablet! It's gone; and so is he!' But two days later apples were again missing or nibbled as before. In vain were other tablets deployed. Our friend evidently said 'I think that white thing must have disagreed with me, I shan't eat another.' And he did not. A fresh place had to be found for the apples.

It has been observed that whereas the cricket field is disfigured by wormcasts our own lawns are free from them. Under correction, I have suggested that this freedom is due entirely to the endless proddings of a troupe of starlings which nest in the studio roof. The birds are indefatigable. Sometimes as many as twenty of them are engaged in systematic research across the big back lawn. As birds among other birds, they are bullies and cowards, charging among sparrows, chaffinches, and the gentle little hedge-warblers with great bustle, but rising in panic at

86

the smallest noise or passing shadow. There can be few more preposterous domestic birds. Rich as their plumage is, they are extraordinarily ungainly, as if their bodies are heavy and the feet at the end of their wide-apart stubby legs are heel-less. They reach the earth with a bump, as crows do; and unlike other birds they give one the impression of needing arms.

But see and hear them in the bird-bath! They have a fury for ablution, clawing away round the edge of the bath, looking nervously all around them, and then hopping into the water and showering fountains of spray. Other starlings join them; there may be as many as three or four in the bath at one time, jostling with passion, dipping their beaks and fluttering their wings as if they could never stop. At last they leap into the air and fly off, only to return and resume the display. By the time baths are over most of the water has gone; but all around the bath is a dripping which lasts for several minutes.

No other birds use the bath so freely. Blackbirds will occasionally hop into the water; but they prefer less public places, and are rather to be seen in the pond or the shallows of a brook than in what to starlings must be the equivalent of a children's bathing pool. Smaller birds hesitate a great deal before they hop in, and even then are soon out again; most of them do no more than sip a little water and do some preening. Only starlings plunge as boys do into the sea.

They are friendless birds. Their especially copious excretions are unpopular; and they behave as if they knew that every man's hand will be against them. Whereas blackbirds and robins, when met in a path, will do no more than move aside (the blackbirds impatiently) they swirl to a distance. Once far away, they hunt for leather-jackets, pausing only to utter the long-drawn whistle that makes them sound like boys incredulous of a tall story. Clever mimics of other birds, they chatter like hens when roosting; but after they seem to have settled for the night, which they do early as if they feared the dark and its dangers, they often interrupt this croodling and snuffling with this same long whistle: 'Whe-e-ee!'

I know something of this, because I hear them in the studio roof. I know when they come home; for they all talk at once, and flutter their wings, and tramp about. At the appropriate season they carry on large-scale building operations, hammering and making long scything noises, and apparently dragging heavy objects from place to place. It is as if they had found their way into a loft where disused suitcases are kept, and wished to clear spaces for their family, or as if they prepared bunks for an immense army. Perhaps it is an immense army? By comparison, I am as silent as a mouse, unless I can bear no more, when I rise up and seize a long pole with which I bang the ceiling.

This causes a breath-holding silence for a few minutes, after which the racket is continued, with less vehemence. At last all activity stops. Darkness falls on the garden. I work in peace, until I am wholly absorbed in my task. But suddenly there is commotion overhead. Somebody has fallen out of his bunk, or has had a bad dream. A crash is followed by much squawking from one bird and much gobbling protest from parents or brothers and sisters, and, of course a muted whistle— 'Whe-e-ee!' Further trampling precedes another silence. We all, myself included, settle once more.

If the disturbance occurs at a late hour, when a tired writer is over-strained, it can be quite frightening. Concentration becomes impossible; and the ensuing silence is uncanny enough to produce shivering. Do birds suffer from nightmare? Is the rumpus due simply to loss of balance? I cannot tell.

How different all this is from the modest tranquillity of wrens and hedge-warblers, who seem never to quarrel, but only to slip about noiselessly in the hedges or on the ground, picking up objects so minute that they are invisible to the human eye, and declaring their presence alone by those brief, tiny, trilling bursts of song which lift the heart. I prefer the little birds; but I admit to finding starlings the most attractively idiosyncratic characters to fly among our banks and trees. They steal nothing;

they are industrious; their uncouthness is more than atoned for by their peacock-iridescent plumage. Long may they continue to whistle, prod, bathe, and bustle!

FIVE

Doctors

I SHOULD HAVE expected such a place as our village to be a model of healthfulness; and so, for many, it is. Octogenarians, including myself, abound. Several nonagenarians have shown that long life is no hindrance to the spirit of youth. In the course of long residence, however, I have found that, as in every other community, illness plays its part.

I have constantly missed familiar faces for weeks at a time, only to learn, when they have been seen again, that the owners have been ill, or in hospital, or that surgical operations have been necessary. Worse still, inquiry has revealed the fact that death is as busy here as elsewhere. A brown face, tanned by exposure to wind and sun, is no guide to what is happening within the body, where a thousand growths or lesions may accumulate or widen, gradually, until one day there is pain, or a thrombosis, or a rupture. A man may be striding across the Common one day, and the next he is in bed with mounting temperature and choking breath. It is an appalling thought, which occurs to me every time I pass two women chatting in the High Street and hear one of them say: 'Doctor says . . .'

When we first arrived, there were three busy and popular doctors, one of whom, retiring nearly twenty years later, and going to Scotland in order to indulge perpetually in his favourite pastime of golf, set a good example to us all by living to be ninety. The others, both younger, took a fresh partner, and carried on as before. They sent their patients to the excellent village hospital, or, alternatively, to the nearest town, where at least three larger hospitals, one of them staffed by nuns, gave devoted service, as they still do. The patients were borne thither by our own ambulance, manned by other villagers; and they were brought home again in the same conveyance, restored to health. This was highly satisfactory. At that time there was no Whitehall dictatorship.

The three doctors who are active today (with the recent addition of a fourth) are not those I first knew. The senior among them, who as a youngster was playing cricket only the other day—was it after all, only the other day? Days are no more to me now than a long moment of childhood—received a tribute in my chance hearing not long ago. Two middle-aged women were deep in conversation as I passed them; and I heard one say, not, on this occasion, 'Doctor says,' but 'What I feel about Doctor D—— is, he's always so *fatherly!*'

I was taken aback; for one who finds it hard to believe that other men also pass a birthday every year continues to see them as they were at a first acquaintance. But the observation was extremely pleasant. It testified to the doctor's personality, and illustrated the goodwill prevailing to this day among those who, in a small community, see doctors, clergymen, labourers, or gardeners, as individuals, and judge them as such.

In cities, however able, however kind, doctors are more remote. They must constantly be called upon to examine and advise strangers whom they never saw before and may never see again. Their prescriptions, especially when the men and women in their surgeries are tongue-tied or secretive, must be based on general medical knowledge and a quick assessment of symptoms. Doctors have not time, in many instances, to acquire all the information needed for profound diagnosis. They do a splendid job, and some, I know, have a genius for enticing patients into the necessary candours. But what patients some of them have!

How different it is in a village, where they go in and out of houses without ceremony, and already know a thousand details about the invalids. Some are really old friends. Some they first saw as babies. They do not need charts to tell of past medical history; it is within memory, as is the medical history of parents, and sometimes grandparents.

I do not know, for they are very discreet, what private views our doctors hold of those who run to them incessantly for certificates and the treatment of minor complaints. I do know—especially now that I must annually be declared fit to drive a car—that they are never perfunctory, nor obviously in a hurry; and that their approach is uniformly humane. This approach is essential in a village doctor. If he were not regarded as a trusted friend he would lose a substantial part of his power to cure. An impatient listener would never do. Nor would any air of being a Medicine Man, who pretends to mysterious knowledge. Our doctors are seen too nearly, and discussed too candidly, to be mysterious characters. Their very hobbies are known to all, and sometimes smiled at; but so are the men themselves, with affection.

Forty-odd years ago, an earlier doctor was spoken of by old villagers, in company with a former rector, an archdeacon, in such a way as to show that these two men had almost legendary quality. Their names were pronounced with reverence; and the doctor, riding everywhere on horseback, was a familiar figure in the district. His successor, that one who became a nonagenarian, was the first I saw. He was a quiet, strolling man, often about the Common, who had been driven in a horse-carriage until shortly before our arrival; and when cars became common his coachman, as serene and fresh-complexioned as his master, had adapted himself to the times and learned to drive a car at a truly dignified pace. One imagined him clucking to the gears and giving them encouragement with a shake of the reins. He said little; but he managed the doctor's small garden and kept the car spotless. He and his master were a well-matched pair, typical of their age.

To the best of my recollection the doctor came only three times to the cottage, always to see my wife. On the first occasion he listened to what she had to say, and replied with brief geniality: 'You've given me a very good description of nettle-rash.' On the second, equally brief and equally genial, he said: 'You're going to have a baby.' On the third, summoned very early in the morning, he took her instantly to the village hospital, where a girl baby arrived soon afterwards. It was not his fault, nor that of his colleagues, that the child was lost: the fault lay with negligence elsewhere.

As he wasted no words, so, without being abrupt, he wasted no time. His decisions were confident and immediate. My own contacts with him were passing encounters near his home, when beginning with the merest 'good days', he by degrees allowed himself more pointed comments upon individuals. These, in which we agreed, showed him to be a man who estimated character at a glance, without sentiment.

Of his two juniors one, a very tall and strikingly handsome man who took long plunging strides, told me that his only medical ambition had been to be a good general practitioner. He could have specialised; but the specialist, he felt, lost contact with ordinary life. A g.p. was of more positive use to his fellow-creatures—whom he loved. This doctor planned—it was his subsidiary ambition—to spend his fortunate years of retirement in reading all the history of mankind that he could compass, a plan which showed how determined he was to keep his noteworthy freshness of mind. One saw him swinging, stethoscope in hand, across the Common on foot, and being waylaid by patients to whom he bent down in close attention. He was stopped once by a very anxious young woman (I thought probably the mother of a sick child) to whom he said a few words, taking her elbow lightly as he spoke, of encouragement. She turned away, anxiety relieved, her step so light that she seemed almost to skip. He had given her, in that one sentence, and by his obvious understanding of her trouble, the reassurance she needed. It was a charming sight, which I shall never forget.

One of this doctor's ex-colleagues at Guy's, who had specialised in obstetrics and was the author of standard books on his subject, spoke warmly of him, declaring that as a medical student he was the wittiest of them all. This other doctor said that if he had wished he could have enjoyed a great career. Having chosen otherwise, he was greatly trusted, and loved by all except the two or three whom he found frowsting in rooms with closed windows. These, wedded to frowst, considered him a little sharp in tone.

Of the third doctor, a man directly descended from the alienist summoned to attend King George the Third during his supposed madness (modern doctors have made a new diagnosis; by which they show that the King, quite sane, suffered from an extremely painful complaint which they called Porphyria; but in the eighteenth century medicine was less subtle than it is now), I have a different memory. The mental picture shows him on a bicycle which he steered with one hand while carrying two violin cases under his other arm. As this suggests, his hobby was music. It did not prevent him from being both a highly skilled doctor and a delightful talker on other subjects; but as recreation it satisfied all his needs.

He was struck by the account given in one of my novels of a man whose illness ended, if I remember rightly, in delusions. It was the most accurate description possible, he insisted, of the inevitable stages of some disease which he named but which I cannot now recall. I assured him that I had invented the character and his illness; but in spite of all, he maintained his commendation. I was almost persuaded that Lord Horder, a master of diagnosis, had whispered directions to me in my sleep.

Naturally, the doctor, after reading my novel, became very friendly. He must have been one of the few people who do not forget, in speaking to me, that I am a writer. I know this, because once, when he wanted to speak of Philip Gibbs, who lived three miles away, he referred to him as 'the other one', meaning that both Gibbs and I were what the village bookshop describes (though for some reason the card is never put alongside a book of my own) as 'local authors'. I profited greatly from his kindness, as the following story will show:

During the Second War, Franz Osborn, the pianist, lived in our village, fulfilling his professional engagements in London, but always returning home at night. Music was his bond with the doctor. Now one midnight Osborn was stranded far away by the inclemency of a German bombing raid. Trains were stopped; and, having no means of getting home, he was desperate. At last he thought of the doctor, to whom he telephoned an appeal, crying: 'Do, for God's sake, my friend, come and rescue me!'

'I will,' replied the doctor, roused from sleep and facing a long drive on sidelights through an inky countryside. 'But it will cost you a hell of a lot of piano-playing.'

'Yes, yes, yes. Certainly! I'll promise anything! Only come and rescue me.'

The doctor set out at once. Osborn was collected and brought to his own door. And in due course he kept his promise.

As a privilege which I shall never forget, I was invited to share the treat. I stumbled through the darkness to a house I did not know, was greeted and led within; and then, for it was a summer night, the doctor and I sat under a tree in the garden while the *maestro* entertained us from indoors, beyond open French windows.

I now have no recollection of what music was played; it was classical, and probably the work of Brahms and Schumann. But for two hours imminent air raids and all other wartime ills were forgotten in an atmosphere of old Germany. I will not say

95

that we drank beer from steins, although there was certainly liquid refreshment of some kind. And it was only afterwards that I realised the irony of a situation in which, while Hitler's Germans were bombing not far away, we should have been listening in tranquillity to music written and first heard in a Germany exalted by romantic idealism.

SIX

'Characters'

Having spoken of the doctors I must proceed to mention some of those whom even doctors here have not been able to keep alive for ever.

Whether he was, or was not, the oldest man in the village, I do not know. He used to sit with some cronies on a seat in front of the cottage whenever cricket was in progress. He was very small, shaven, but always with a white bristle on his chin, and intensely amused by the mishaps to be expected when running men trip and stumble. Then his aged laugh would cackle loudly, and he would shout unintelligibly at the victim. He liked to see catches made in the long field, and when a big hit was made he had only a single cry. It was 'Run it eaut!' Those, owing to his lack of teeth, were the only words I distinguished. He had a surname, of course; but was always called 'Daddy'. I think he must have been a man of considerable age.

Two others, younger in those days than Daddy, lived to be nonagenarians; and I still regret the loss of both of them. The first, short, fresh-coloured, sturdy, rather stout, white-moustached, full-chinned, and always wearing a half-secret and half-roguish smile, was by occupation a bricklayer. He was very religious, and on a more mundane level took great pride in his skill as an erector of chimneys. Heights, he boasted, had no terror for him; he had One Above who would always assure that he did not fall.

The second, a year younger, had been his schoolmate, and was a much slighter figure, also fresh-coloured, very dapper, and although with a slight country accent precise in speech. He always wore bright flowers in his buttonhole, and always, I think, a smart brown suit. The two, being ancient, would sit side by side under the maple trees, exchanging news and reminiscences in high good humour.

Both had extremely good memories of local happenings over the past three-quarters of a century. The remarkable difference between them was that the elder, when dating an event, would say 'That happened about nineteen hundred and one,' while his junior, ever more exact, would say, smacking his lips: 'September twentieth, nineteen-two.' His friend never questioned the revision. He felt real admiration for his junior's (by a year) exactitude. He would even refer one to the friend, as being more reliable than himself, and always spoke of him as 'Mister L——'.

I knew the older man better. That was because he first came to the cottage on some job of repairs, and afterwards, when forbidden in his late seventies to climb long ladders to reach his beloved chimneys, because he helped us by digging in the garden, which he did until he decided that his other, and gratuitous, digging engagements kept him fully occupied.

Digging came second to chimney-building among his favourite occupations; and he dug the gardens of his widowed neighbours until the end of his life. If he came to help us, although always ready for conversation when the work was done, he never paused in his steady occupation. He then, being used to speaking extempore in chapel, showed a fine narrative and rhetorical gift. He never hesitated for a word, but told his stories and made his ripostes, slowly indeed, yet with model brevity. Always with that secret smile of inner amusement.

In youth he had been in the habit of walking ten miles to work and ten miles home again, and would then, un-tired, attend a prayer meeting. Once he and some fellow-members of his congregation decided to spend a day by the sea. They prayed overnight for fine weather. In the morning clouds were low and the outlook gloomy. The old man's housekeeper (for his wife had become ill and incapable of running the home) said, with reference to the threat of rain, 'Hadn't you better take your mackintosh?' He, with a fine mixture of faith and humour, replied: 'No. To do that, after praying for good weather, would seem to show distrust of Our Lord.'

Relating the story, he omitted to tell me whether it rained.

On another occasion I had been digging a bank in the garden which was solid with white clay. My progress was so slow that our gardener offered to finish the job. I fear he did not think highly of me as a digger; and in fact he was also critical of the old man, whom he described as 'a dirty' (meaning rough) digger. Towards the evening he finished the job, and as I happened to pass at the final moment I congratulated him. He admitted that he wished he had left it to me, after all.

We were discussing the bank's stubborn nature when our friend, on his way home, joined us. I mentioned the clay. 'Ah,' said he, having had an easier task; 'not like what I've been a-digging in the front garden, then.' I said 'What you've been digging has been dug for generations. Probably by the Ancient Britons.' 'Well,' was his reply, 'one of them has been digging it today.'

He was merry, and active, to the end. Having no chimneys to build, but retaining his confidence in heights, he volunteered to pick apples from a big tree in the neighbourhood, reared his long ladder, and went up to the highest branches. Alas, the ladder slipped. The anxiety which had made his former employers dissuade him from chimney work was justified. He fell to the ground. He always maintained that he had suffered no injury, and made light of the incident. But it was ominous. Another fall, this time downstairs, at home, was too much for him, and broken ribs had their consequences.

I only heard of these a little while afterwards. I also heard that there was great hesitation over telling his friend and schoolmate of the old man's death, in case it should be too severe a shock for one who was already beginning to ail. At last younger members of his family broke the news. It was received in complete silence. The survivor sat as if stunned. Only after several minutes did he betray life-long rivalry, by remarking, in a tone of quiet complacency: 'I've beat him, then.'

It is sometimes believed, and the foregoing may have seemed to confirm the view, that 'characters' (who are assumed to be eccentrics) have disappeared from the English scene. This is not true. There will always be 'characters'. True, we now have synthetic types, who seek by clothing or hair styles to make themselves appear to be 'different' from the majority; but they will not pass the test I apply. To me, a real 'character' is a person outside the common run, who is quite unaware of his own peculiarity. He believes himself to be ordinary, and supposes others to be the same. You remember how exultant Bernard Shaw was when told by an occulist that he had normal sight. The occulist vainly reminded him that very few men had 'normal' sight; he applied the term to his whole outlook, on the ground that in the country of the blind a one-eyed man is King. He was assuredly a King; and we shall not look on his like again. My real criticism of modern eccentrics is that they follow a particular and not very admirable fashion. This fashion may change tomorrow; and they will be out of it. If they knew more of history, they would find that what they think new, or bold, and very striking, has all been done before, and like other fashions has passed. This applies to artistic experiments, as well as to locks, skirts, and paint. Genuine originality is not eccentric, nor a thing of fashion. It is, as William Hazlitt said, 'any conception of things, taken immediately from nature, and neither borrowed from nor common to, others. . . . It is feeling the ground sufficiently firm under one's feet to be able to go alone.'

That is to say, it is entirely un-self-conscious. The originals I have known, from Arnold Bennett to Walter de la Mare and Siegfried Sassoon, have been men entirely without affectation. They have had foibles; Bennett certainly enjoyed the laughter produced by his stammered comments; but their minds were too deeply reflective to allow of pose. Speaking of the persons described in his own works, another original, Henry James, confessed that 'my identity for myself was *all* in my sensibility to their exhibition, *with not a scrap left over for a personal show.*'

The later age, with its organised advertising, is adverse to this simplicity. The saintly are dug out of retirement and encouraged into the deadly light of exhibitionism. Once they know they have attracted attention, the most modest can hardly escape spoiling. They insensibly cultivate their most admired mannerisms, and in time become bores and are cast aside.

This happened, or seemed to happen, with Bernard Shaw, Thomas Beecham, and Oscar Wilde, all of whom were natural wits. Wilde grew affected, Shaw gave outrageous advice to the young in order to shock their parents. Beecham could not restrain the expected retorts. They are still remembered as personalities; and it is not until we recall their work that we realise how keenly, under the veneer, they respected their art. Then, indeed, we find that Shaw, for all his knockabout, was a man of convictions; Wilde, ostracised by Society for a homosexuality which has become fashionable, an inventor whose wit rarely betrayed him into malice; and Beecham nobly determined, in an age when pretentiousness demanded that one should care only for 'the first rate', to produce light opera and perform light music. These facts prove that they were not spoiled by the cackle of the superficial.

Meanwhile, however, they had ceased to be 'characters'. They had all succumbed to the artificiality of the sophisticated world. Whether this made them better known, or more influential, or as performers more expert, I am not concerned to say.

If I had collected 'characters', I should now display them. I have not done so, and I do not do so. In the course of a long life, however, I have found and loved a number, of whom I wish to speak. They have included authors, journalists, architects, solicitors, chemists, and schoolmasters, all marked by the simplicity I demand. My own mother, for instance, combined innocence with a belief that she was full of craft. It was a particularly innocent craft, without a tincture of evil. She never lied; she never punished; I never knew her to say or think a malicious thing. Having education, talent, and delightful humour, she was condemned by circumstance to be a household drudge; but she was so unselfish that she never troubled about the drudgery. Instead, after being widowed at the age of forty-five, she devoted herself to her two sons, and submitted (as they grew older, and began to lead independent lives) to their affectionate teasing with an equanimity which, if she had been serious, would have appeared saintly.

She was not serious. She had great pride in her two boys; but not in any worldly success they might achieve. She claimed to know all their faults, and I believe she did so. She insisted on their qualities. The household was always a merry one. It was never sentimental. It was she, when we were young, who warned us against retaliation for ills inflicted by others with a single unforgotten remark. This was: 'Two wrongs don't make a right.' It was she who observed that 'toast's the grub that makes the butter fly.' And it was she who said to myself, 'I always feel sure you must be nice, because you have such nice friends.' By 'nice' she meant nothing priggish; but only that whatever was silly or irreverent in my nature was not vicious. Her standard of truthfulness was absolute; and neither my brother nor I, both of us highly inventive, dreamed of telling her a lie. In fact she was my notion of a 'character', small, modest, determined, selfless, and a darling.

SEVEN

Literary 'Characters'

THE FIRST literary 'character' I ever knew was a journalist
and editor (he was also a minor poet; best known for his
indefatigable journalism) named St John Adcock. I forget when
I first met him; but we were friends, certainly, from 1912 until
his death in the early 'thirties. He had the most singular half-
closed eyes I ever saw, and as he was in the habit of smoking
cigarettes endlessly as he typed I always thought the eyes had
been closed in defence against the drifting smoke. He had a
completely silent laugh; and his kindness to the lame literary
dogs by whom every editor is surrounded was such that his
hand was never out of his pocket. This kindness affected his
literary pronouncements, and he praised many who were un-
deserving of his praise. As is common with such men, he worked
himself to death.

The other day I came across a sort of *dossier* containing many
of his letters to me about one of these literary lame dogs, a man
who wrote one good book in the 'nineties, threw up a regular
job in order to devote himself to literature, and was reduced,
first to the composition of unsuccessful pot-boilers, and then to

a species of begging. Several collections were made on his behalf by fellow-writers, and, as was to be expected, Adcock befriended him for years. At last, with immense effort, he set in motion a project for getting the steady drinker a Civil List Pension.

The pension was granted by Stanley Baldwin; but Baldwin, having learned of the lame dog's habits, stipulated that it should not be paid direct. He invited Adcock to be the administrator. Adcock, I think fearing that he would be unable to resist an almost daily clamour, asked if I might be joined with him in the task. It was agreed. Hence the *dossier*. It is a most remarkable collection of letters, showing the difficulty experienced by two men at grips with the ingenuities of a victim of 'the demon drink'. We doled; we delayed; we haggled; but the pensioner, knowing that we had money in a joint account, was full of pretexts. First he needed a typewriter, and then new clothes. He was ill; he was starving; his wife was ill and unhappy; and whatever we allowed him went straight into the pockets of publicans. In vain did Adcock shelter himself by pleading that I was a hard man; he was not believed. The appeals continued until our funds were greatly reduced, and we were desperate.

And all the time Adcock, who was directly pestered, managed to laugh, managed to treat the problem as one, not for exasperation, not for despair, but as a delightful conspiracy between us two for the protection of an incorrigible child. He never failed in kindness or patience, although he was perfectly informed of all that happened. I suspect that he secretly gave money of his own; but the *dossier* is free from cynicism because his heart was light and his sympathy for all lame literary dogs was inexhaustible.

Our trial ended when the torment had a tipsy fall outside a hospital and did not survive medical attention. We paid for his funeral, and wound up our trust. But the insight I gained into Adcock's nature fixed him in my mind for all time as a 'character' of the sweetest variety, a man who went to endless trouble for others, and never once thought of his own convenience or his own personality. This was a 'character' indeed.

Arnold Bennett was another, as I have said; but I have written elsewhere of him, as I have done of Walter de la Mare and Siegfried Sassoon. Neither de la Mare nor Sassoon ever visited our cottage, and they do not, therefore, enter the country picture. One who was a frequent visitor, because he lived only three miles away and in growing old came to regard us as reliable and appreciative friends, was Philip Gibbs. When lonely, he would without hesitation telephone asking us to visit him, or asking if he might visit us. He said in one of his auto-biographical volumes that we were almost the only literary friends he retained; and in time he became one of the dozen or so men with whom, from boyhood onward, I have talked without reserve.

The relationship was the more remarkable because I had previously formed from reading his novels the impression that he was a facile sentimentalist who, in his celebrated novel, *The Street of Adventure*, had travestied the journalist's occupation. As a precocious young man, he had been employed on a short-lived Liberal newspaper called *The Tribune* which tried at great expense to do for London what *The Manchester Guardian* was doing for the world. His writings in *The Tribune*, ranging from news stories to literary criticism of no quality, appeared daily and were read disapprovingly by myself in the first flush of juvenile severity. *The Street of Adventure* purported to tell the inside story of this paper, and to show how its death tragically affected the lives of those involved in the ruin. The book attracted much attention, and I believe caused the author to be sued for libel by a fellow-journalist; but it was painfully sentimental, and persuaded others, as well as myself, that Gibbs was altogether superficial.

Gibbs's cousin, Mary Agnes Hamilton, in the course of an autobiographical study, remarked as his misfortune that he had no brains. It was a severe condemnation, especially coming from one whom I had always considered something of a woolly-wits; but Gibbs took it in good part, and cheerfully repeated the verdict in conversation, making no protest and no adverse comment on his critic. This showed that by my definition he was a 'character'. Nevertheless I long continued to think Mrs Hamilton's verdict just.

I first met Gibbs, I think, at one of the dinner parties given in London by the American publisher, George Doran; but he was also a member of the Reform Club, where I remember that he was scornfully dismissed by J. A. Spender, editor of *The Westminster Gazette,* and a member, with Gibbs, of an official disarmament committee, as 'one of these novelists'. I ventured to remind Spender that I, too, was *'one of these novelists'*; but the objection was brushed aside, as if he thought my other writings, or perhaps my conversation, which he enjoyed, excused an indulgence in abominable craft. At any rate, Gibbs was condemned. I am sorry to say that I made no effort to protest against the condemnation.

And then, when we were established in our cottage, I met him in the village, and our friendship began. By degrees my opinion of the man changed completely. I still thought his writing was done too easily, and with too little thought, as if he tapped out a stream of words in which he converted recently current events into novels without critical depth; but in talk he was a different man, wise, shrewd, and extraordinarily charming.

This leads me to say, not that one should always know a writer personally before judging his work; but that very often the author does injustice to his natural gifts when he sits down, pen in hand, or, as Gibbs did, with a typewriter before him. The work should be judged as work; but I have known other men, more gifted than Gibbs, whose work lacks the lustre of a strong personality. One misses the voice, the laughter, and the vivid animation of manner which is to be found only in listening to what arouses spontaneous exchange.

When Gibbs talked, he was the experienced man of the world, seeing mankind in remarkable focus, without illusion. His humour—quite absent from his novels—was remarkable. He could dismiss a pretentious stylist with one devastating word ('Thesaurus'), estimate a talent (for example, of a modern writer, 'his first book was fair; his second poor; his third no good at all'), with quiet certainty, and judge a man with charity but cautious realism. When he wrote, he fell into the conventions of popular story-telling. If his work is ever consulted by some future historian, it may offer occasional sidelights upon contemporary manners or events; he would have been the last person to claim any other merit for it.

Modesty was instinctive in Gibbs. When he learned that in an American Television quiz the question was asked 'Who was Sir Philip Gibbs?' he told the story with innocent amusement, ignoring the fact that during the First World War his name was known to all as that of one of the most widely-read correspondents at the Front, and that his novels had enjoyed as tremendous a popularity in the United States as in Britain. No hint of reproach to a public which had turned to other idols was ever communicated in that deep and aristocratic voice (which he called 'sepulchral'); and he had no alarms about his ability to endure a neglected future. He was a journalist and talker, with a quick eye for picturesque fact, and a repertory of anecdotes second, in my experience, to none.

Gibbs was not my notion of a countryman. He was always scrupulously dressed, as if for the West End; and with a hat worn at a slight angle looked more like a distinguished actor than a bucolic. He was decidedly handsome, and his manner indicated a precise courtesy more proper to a diplomat than to the rough and tumble of journalism. Perhaps he was a diplomat in domestic affairs. The courtesy certainly was not assumed. It led him in one instance, as I shall relate, into something like cowardice.

Lady Gibbs was a wise and delightful woman, who watched

tirelessly over his health and well-being. She was his beloved protectress (all women instinctively 'mothered' him), who in his eyes only had one fault, which was really his own fault. He had once allowed himself, I suppose from a wish to show appreciation, to praise some kippered herrings. That was encouragement enough for a wife who wished to indulge his every fancy. She instantly assumed that kippers were among his favourite foods.

I learned these facts when I came across Gibbs, on a Winter afternoon, hovering near our railway station. Thinking him less cheerful than usual, I said 'What are you doing here, standing about in the cold?' His reply was: 'My dear feller, my wife has gone to buy me some kippers.' He then told the story, concluding with much laughter: 'And I *hate* the things!' He was too kind and polite ever to reveal the truth to Lady Gibbs; and the eating of kippers became one of his martyrdoms.

After his wife's death Gibbs spent a number of years in kipperless and well-tended widowerhood, troubled only by cataract in both eyes and the respiratory complaint of which he died. He bore every ill with calm, and patiently waited until the cataract operation could be performed. That took place in central London at the height of the Second War, and I visited him in hospital. He was being looked after by some of the most beautiful nurses I have ever seen. I spoke of their beauty.

'Are they beautiful?' asked Gibbs. 'I can't see them. They're very kind.'

He then told how, at night during air-raids, all the nurses (and I hope their patients) assembled round his bed, while he distracted them from thoughts of danger with stories of his encounters with men and women in many lands, and in both war and peace.

He did not pretend to be intrepid; but he must have been so. A very fire-eating war correspondent named H. W. Nevinson insisted during the recovery of Ostend in World War I that they should walk up and down the plage together while the town was under fire. 'To show the Germans we're not afraid.' 'But I *am* afraid,' protested Gibbs. Nevertheless he walked up and down with his gigantic friend.

Still imperturbable, and wanting at the age of seventy-five to know what it felt like, he arranged to companion a test pilot from the local airfield in what was then the latest experimental jet plane. Some would have found the journey terrifying; Gibbs greatly enjoyed it, flying and wheeling without qualm at five hundred miles an hour. Being a journalist, he turned the trip to account. That was his purpose. Latterly, however, he did not like to be described as a journalist; the term reminded him too much of early days (which of course he made amusing in narrative) when he had been dismissed at a moment's notice by, successively, Alfred Harmsworth and C. Arthur Pearson. In the latter case he had just refused to write an article acclaiming Bacon as the author of Shakespeare's plays. 'I didn't believe he was,' said Gibbs.

The stories he told the nurses included many that I heard in forty years of friendship. Some were extraordinary, even macabre; others so simple that they needed his voice and narrative skill to give them charm. He claimed to have over-reached Arnold Bennett in buying the copyright of *The Grand Babylon Hotel* for Tillotson's Newspaper Syndicate; and he said that Bennett, afterwards realising the truth, warned all writers against the arts of 'a pale young man with nicotine-stained fingers'. He also described how, at some Royal garden party, he nimbly eluded a rope with which officials were separating great from common people (the French Ambassador being less fortunate), and found himself walking within a yard of Queen Alexandra. The Queen, imagining him to be at least a peer, addressed him, and, being very deaf, was so pleased at being able to hear his mighty voice that ever afterwards she greeted him as an old friend.

I have told in another book how this voice, in which as we sat together in a taxi to Waterloo he told me the story of his conversations with Ethel le Neve, Dr Crippen's girl friend, penetrated the din of London's traffic and reached the ears of the driver. It was a fascinating story; and the driver was so enchanted that as I paid him he cried enthusiastically: 'Thank you, sir. And I hope you'll have a *very* happy journey!'

The journey was indeed happy; but at the end of it we found our bus full. A boy, recognising Gibbs, jumped up to offer his seat; but I was less lucky, and the conductor would not let me stay on board. Gibbs wanted to get out again. Knowing, however, that it was essential for him, in a half-blind state, to reach home in daylight, I waved him back. A relief bus was run. I saw Gibbs enter his own gateway, and was happy. But Gibbs long tormented himself with self-reproach for letting me, as he thought, make a sacrifice on his account; and nothing I could say eased his mind. This concern for another was typical.

He was idolised in his own village, where he was known to everybody and took a paternal interest in all the children. One of the celebrations of his eightieth birthday, in fact, after the local grown-ups had toasted and extolled him, was an immense party in his garden for children and their parents only. I was not present at this, although my own daughter had an exceptional tenderness for Gibbs; but I believe it was triumphant.

The consequence of his friendships with children was a multitude of stories about them. Some related, of course, to those of his own family; but two concerned others in the village. The first was of a little four-year-old boy who ran indoors, white with excitement, to tell his father that a bird in the garden had looked at him with a beady eye and said 'Hullo'. The father pooh-poohed this account, saying 'Nonsense!' However, he was persuaded to go to see the bird; and he, too, was gravely shaken when it looked at him in the same knowing manner and said: 'Good morning. How are you?' Great uneasiness seized him. It was only allayed when the bird was found to be a pet jackdaw straying for a while from its home in another part of the village.

III

The second story was of a boy of eight who took a tremendous liking to a bishop who came to stay with his parents. The bishop so won his heart that when the visit was ending the boy said he wanted to give his new friend a present. What sort of present?' he was asked. 'My Bible.' 'Oh, no,' said the Bishop. 'Don't give me that.' 'Yes, I want to. It's a very nice Bible, with pictures.' He ran upstairs, was absent for several minutes, and returned with the Bible, in which, with some blots, he had written the inscription: 'From the Author.'

Alas! That deep voice will never again be heard in our cottage. It was ever welcome. The affectionate courtesy of Gibbs's manner, and his interest in everything concerning his friends, was so unquestionable that whenever he arrived it was as if we resumed a conversation which had begun overnight. Although he reached the age of eighty, and his step became slower, he showed no sign of mental age; and his death was felt by both my wife and myself as one of the greatest losses we had ever experienced.

EIGHT

In the Train

LET ME now describe another character.
It used to be one of the Englishman's foibles to seek
an empty railway compartment and if possible occupy it alone
for the entire journey. This habit has declined of late, partly because a younger generation prefers group consciousness, partly
because British coach-building has followed American custom
in making a central aisle between the seats. Being old-fashioned,
I still hanker for solitude when travelling. I have never wanted
to talk in trains—I prefer to look out of the window at whatever
we are passing;—and I have never addressed a stranger in the
same compartment.

If all men had been as I am, I should have missed a number
of extraordinarily interesting encounters and communications.
Some, naturally, have been quite conventional; little chats on
topics of the day, desultory observations about Test cricket,
and inquiries about times of arrival, unevennesses of track, and
so on; but those standing out in memory were quite otherwise.

At a time when I travelled regularly every week from our
village to London I often had single fellow-passengers in the

roomy compartments of both the local and the London trains. They almost invariably spoke to me; and I think I know why. When somebody is greatly agitated, or deeply preoccupied with a problem, he feels a desperate need for relief. A stranger who will never be seen again offers the best possible confidant, for he can never taunt the speaker with memory of words unguardedly spoken; and if that stranger is in the same railway carriage on a long or longish journey, time, place, and confessor are all together. The very motion of the carriage is a reassurance; it means that there is a limit to narrative and that the narrative itself cannot be overheard by others.

The smallest excuse will answer the would-be communicant's need—the request for a light, the glimpse of some known face on the receding station platform, a headline in a newspaper;—the rest will follow with ever-increasing assurance and fluency. But I suppose there must be first some inquiring peep at the stranger. If he is a scowler, his blankness would discourage. Apparently I am not a scowler.

As a consequence, I have heard on such journeys the sorrows of a North of England railway guard, condemned by 'the system' to spend four nights a week away from home, wife, and children; the despairs of a Trade Union official over his junior members; the angers of a man whose in-laws had invaded his home; the anxieties of one whose career, once promising, was threatened with collapse; the distraction of a young woman whose husband's ill-health was due to persistence in a diet which killed his father and was doing the same for him; and many more. Strangest of all was a claim to Royal blood.

This last was so astonishing that on returning home that night I set it down in as nearly as possible the very words of the morning. I include my companion among 'characters', because he was gentle, likeable, and unique. I never heard his name, nor knew where he lived, nor saw him again. Listen!

The conversation began easily enough. The train, on a very cold morning, was unheated; and my companion, sitting at the other end of our compartment, launched an attack on the short-comings of British Railways. He was tall, slim, handsome, and middle-aged; obviously a gentleman. His long coat and bowler hat were black; and his smile was benevolent. His manner was very courteous.

I ventured the suggestion, in reply, that some trains were better than others. He agreed, asking whether I had travelled much abroad. I admitted that I had done so. It then appeared that he was well acquainted with the United States, and had a high opinion of the Americans. I said I had a number of American friends, who were all extremely intelligent. I did not mention that they showed this intelligence by being, at least as far as I was concerned, Anglophiles. Instead I took from my case a book which I had intended to read during the journey.

The action was disregarded. My new friend, indeed, appeared not to notice it; for he continued by remarking that in his opinion American business methods were better than our own. Being an expert in Economics, he had long foreseen British inflationary troubles, and in the past had warned the country against them. I said nobody in Britain took any notice of warnings. This led him to ask whether I, too, was an Economist. I said that on the contrary I was that uneconomic person a professional writer.

The news spread a cloud across his handsome face.

'You say "a writer". You don't mean just a *novelist*?' he anxiously inquired.

'I've written some novels,' I admitted. 'But other things too.'

'Not a *journalist*!' he implored.

'Some journalism,' said I.

That was very bad. He spoke sorrowfully of the ignorance of journalists.

'Yes, many of them are very ignorant,' said I, book in hand, thinking that this must bring the conversation to an end. A novelist and a journalist! He seemed to be saying to himself: 'Oh, dear me; I'm disappointed in this fellow. I took him for somebody intelligent!' I opened my book.

There was a moment's pause. Then, apparently, charity appeased his distaste. Leaving the other end of the compartment, he took a seat immediately opposite.

'Are you interested in history?' he abruptly demanded. 'Do you know anything about it?'

'No,' said I. 'I've read a good many histories; but I'm not a scholar.'

'The Stuarts?'

'Only the obvious books.'

He seemed gratified by my confession; or perhaps he thought me over-modest, for he looked searchingly into my face.

'I know a good deal,' he said, at last. 'Indeed, I can tell you some curious facts. You've read ——, ——, and ——?' naming authors whose works, and even names, were unfamiliar to me.

'No. Clarendon, Burnet, Pepys . . .'

These were tolerable enough. They produced a careless nod. The real approach followed.

'You remember how ——' (In the jolting of the train the name did not reach my ears), tells that, when Charles was in Jersey, a young man was with him? That they were inseparable?'

'No, I didn't know.'

'A beautiful young man?'

'No.'

'Well, that young man disappeared. There's no further mention of him at any time. He simply drops out.'

'Extraordinary.'

My friend smiled in delight. He continued to observe me closely. He then said, with an air of triumph:

'The explanation—you understand?—is simply that the beautiful young man was a girl dressed in man's clothing. When she disappeared, it was because she was having a baby. Charles's eldest son.'

'That's remarkable,' said I. 'It's news to me.'

'It's news to most people. But there's no doubt about it. The baby was Charles's eldest son. He grew up. His mother died. He disappeared. What happened to him?'

'I can't imagine.'

'He was called James de la Cloche. You can read something of him in Acton. It's quite inaccurate.'

'I seem to remember something in Acton. One of the essays?'

'Yes, one of the essays. It tells how Charles called him "Prince James Stuart". You remember?'

'I've forgotten.'

My friend leaned forward.

'He took Orders. He came secretly to England in sixteen sixty-eight; and was sent to Rome on a mission. That's the crux of the matter. He disappeared. And why did he disappear? I'll tell you. James was really his murderer. He betrayed the boy to Louis the Fourteenth, who had him kidnapped. He was the Man in the Mask.'

'Good heavens!'

'The whole point was that the moment Charles died he was to be killed, so that James could succeed. Have you read anything about the Man in the Mask?'

'Fifty years ago I read a book by Andrew Lang.'

'Oh, yes. Yes, I know that book. It's not the real story, of course. Lang knew nothing. No, there are secret papers that make it quite clear. Unquestionably authentic.'

His smiling joy in my astonishment was delightful. Having paused for greater effect, he resumed:

'I never gave the matter a thought until—a good many years ago—when my father died—after the funeral, I was sitting by the fire—looked up—and saw—Charles!'

It dawned on me that we had deserted the documents and were in the world of visitations. We were also outside the range of the '15 and the '45. This was a Jacobite story.

'Really?' said I. 'How remarkable! Did he say anything?'

'No. He was just there. Quite unmistakable. It set me thinking. I thought "Why?" I began to study the secret history. I realised . . . There's no doubt whatever. I have all the essential information. The estate's in Chancery. The facts are quite familiar to —— and —— (naming dignitaries then living). They all know.'

'And say nothing?'

'They say nothing.'

'But isn't that immoral?'

He smiled with enjoyment of my simplicity.

'Nothing's impossible to these people. The truth passes secretly from generation to generation. The father swears his son to secrecy. Nothing's said. Nothing's allowed to be said. But it's true, you see.'

'Will it never come out?' I asked.

My friend smiled once more. His smile had a singular quality such as I have seen only once or twice in my life, once on the face of an ardent Baconian.

'You remember the incident at Ascot? When the flag opposite the Royal Enclosure was struck by lightning? It was the Standard of Scotland. That was a sign. There have been others. Oh, innumerable others. They built a house. The night before they came to occupy it the house was destroyed. They built another. The same thing happened. That will go on and on. You can't defy Providence indefinitely; it's impossible.'

'Indeed, it appears to be,' said I. 'Who are "they"?'

He gave me a still more extraordinary glance, and lowered his voice.

'These people.'

I wrestled with the implication that august names could not be pronounced. My companion added:

'I'm the direct descendant of that girl in Jersey. There's no question about it. The evidence is conclusive. I've shown it to several experts. They all agree.'

'But this is sensational!' I said.

He shrugged.

'Oh,' said he; 'I don't want the throne. We've had all that. There's nothing in it.'

'Hard work?' I suggested. 'No privacy?'

'Nothing in it. I wouldn't choose . . .'

The train stopped. The platform was beside us. We had reached our journey's end in magically brief time. My friend smiled again. As we stepped out on to the platform he saw that I had dropped my ticket, courteously stooped and restored it to me as if he had been a mere commoner, said 'goodbye', and disappeared into the crowd.

Isn't that a strange story? Does it not show that men who are silent in crowds are drawn to communicate their secret thoughts to strangers sitting alone with them in railway compartments? And that the world, if only we would believe it, is full of marvels?

NINE

Our Gardener

I REFER NOW to a character who had not the wide acquaintance of Philip Gibbs, but who enjoyed the affection and respect of all who knew him. This was our gardener, whom I have already mentioned. I have told of his punctuality and reluctance to go home; but have not yet described him.

He was fairly tall, thin, large-footed, and moderately dark; and he wore a small, steadily greying moustache. One of his eyes had at some time been damaged by a blow from a tennis ball; but his sight was good. He always wore a cloth cap, and although often invited to do so by our female staff refused to wear a gardener's apron. He kept methodically, day by day, a diary which I had to buy him every year, recording in it not only such things as 'plant carrots' but the state of the weather and any details such as the visit of a strange bird or the illness of a chicken. If the temperature rose, he liked to write the words 'Great heat'; otherwise his account of it was genial and pleasantly reserved.

Other people used sometimes to write in this diary, mentioning for example, that they had heard the cuckoo. He ignored all such frivolous claims, and the arrival had no official recognition until he was able to write (which he did in larger letters than usual) 'Hear cuckoo.' After that there could be no question. The cuckoo had arrived.

When we began to keep chickens he attended to their comfort, and when, as a little girl, my daughter kept three guinea-pigs which had been given to her by a boy, it was he who made cages for them, supplied unlimited hay for their comfort, and cleaned the cages conscientiously each morning so that although they were indoors they were always sweet. The pigs themselves responded by showing considerable affection. They would rush out of their bedrooms on to what we called their balconies, and would nibble fingers or waistcoat buttons with the greatest confidence. If they were taken for a run in the garden, he kept a paternal eye on their proceedings, and at last brought them indoors again in a large trug basket.

One of the chickens was his favourite because, through some malformation, she became too crippled to run. She would hide under a cabbage, or in long grass; and when we passed without seeing her would give a little croodle to invite attention and receive a pat. The gardener loved Crips, as we called her, and carried her back to the run every evening before he went home. Unfortunately an unknown dog found his way into the garden and chased Crips, who could not escape. Rescue was immediately organised; Crips was physically unharmed; but the fright had been too much for her, and she died in my daughter's arms. The gardener was so distressed that as he told the story of what had happened his eyes were moist.

His devotion to my daughter was complete. When very tiny, she would join him in the garden, or would visit his shed for perhaps half-an-hour at a time; and when she decided to return to the house she would make the journey perched on his shoulder. Because he knew that this would give her pleasure, he one day trundled her all the way to the village and back in his wheelbarrow; and it was on this same wheelbarrow, several years afterwards, that he collected from the railway station on her birthday a big doll's house which I had managed overnight to bring so far, by other transport, from London.

The barrow was his friend. It was old, and in spite of being mended and re-painted and re-fitted with a pneumatic tyre it had a familiar rattle. This was what betrayed his movements after dark, when he should have been at home. He used it for all purposes, to carry spade, fork, hoe, and rake, or to bring to the house in winter the logs he had just sawn and split. It is still in use; it still rattles; and as I, in turn, use it for various purposes I am perpetually reminded of its original user and his inexhaustible loyalty.

As an instance of this, I recall that when our first daughter was born he was delighted, saying that she would be just what the household needed. I have already mentioned in writing about the village doctors that the child, through no fault of theirs, received an injury at birth. At first it was thought that the wound would heal; but on the ninth day, a Saturday, I was summoned to the hospital, without being told why I was wanted. Only on arrival there did I learn that she was dead. This, of course, was a great shock; and I stayed for some time with my wife who, although thinking nothing of herself, was really crushed by what was our first unhappiness.

Afterwards I walked home to what I thought would be an empty house. It was not empty. Hearing that I had been sent for, and guessing that the cause must be bad news of some kind, B. had waited for my return, so that I should not be without company in an hour of distress.

He was never obsequious; never argumentative, although he did sometimes rebel against the little plants brought to the cottage by our original housekeeper. One time it was a bush of Old Man, and she told us he had said 'What you old women see in Old Man I can't understand; nasty stinking stuff!' But he tended it carefully. The housekeeper, always amused by him, brought some of her home-made elderberry wine, which she mulled at lunchtime, giving some to us and a glass to him. She was delighted by its effects. She said: 'He liked his wine. His eyes did just sparkle!' Whether this was one of the few occasions when he sang, I do not remember.

Nor do I remember that he and I ever discussed politics; but I should say that he was an independent Tory. He one day remarked of certain contemporary music: 'They call it "syncopated", just as they call chemical manure "synthetic": they're both as far as possible from Nature.' He took a poor view of the song *Land of Hope and Glory*, and when at last he heard grand opera on the Radio he was sadly disappointed. I do not know what his musical taste really was: if he sang a snatch as he walked down a path the sound was like that made by a bumble bee when alarmed or delighted.

His vocabulary, when he relied on natural taste, was exceptionally good, whether in speech or writing (his letters always told exactly what one wanted to know), although he invariably used the countryman's 'were' with the singular pronoun. It was only when he had carelessly read or imperfectly remembered a word from a newspaper that he startled us by speaking of something as 'dilapated' or made 'wanton' sound like 'bantam'.

He was visibly alarmed by my first venture in hedge-clipping; but after I had completed the easiest of all, a privet, he took a long professional squint down it, and said: 'Very good. Did anybody *show* you how to do it?' The question revealed deep scepticism of my gardening capability; or perhaps only a distrust of all amateurs, which is probably common to all craftsmen. Fortunately I have a good eye; and hedge-trimming and fire-lighting are the only arts in which I claim genius. Therefore scepticism passed. I was allowed ever afterwards to clip any hedge I pleased.

I was proud of his approval; for his standards were high. As long as he lived, the garden was both beautiful and well-tended. Alas, at one time he was so ill that he was forced to stay away for a month. Thinking that he would need his wages, I drove to his home and knocked at the door. He rose from bed and

123

tottered to the window, afterwards saying to his wife 'I think it's our car.' Thereupon the front door was opened. After recovery, he no longer cycled to work, but travelled by bus, learning strange facts from fellow-passengers, but no longer able to add to the store of rusty screws, buttons, and minor implements which he had formerly been apt to spy at the roadside.

Illness did not prevent him, when war came, from making a wonderful underground bomb shelter, and, during our absences from home, from keeping everything in perfect trim and staying as late as he chose. All the same, he began to age. His step grew slower. His hands sometimes trembled. To me he always professed himself very well; but he took a longer Summer holiday than before, and went to the seaside.

On one of his holidays, being always interested in other people's gardens, he noticed at the side of a drive some superfine plants. The flowers were of the same kind as some he grew at home; but of a far larger size and richer colour. He was determined to get a cutting; and on the last night of his stay crept up to the gate of the house with theft as his object. A car arriving with its headlights fully on gave him a great fright; but the cutting was secured and taken home in naughty triumph. However, punishment was not escaped. When the flower which had been resplendent in the other garden bloomed in his, it was exactly like all the others.

One evening, as it was getting dark, I heard him near the studio, sweeping up clippings which I had left in the path. Knowing that it was almost time for his homeward bus, I jumped up and went to the door, calling out: 'Don't bother about those, B. Catch your bus. Olivia [our daughter] will sweep them up later.' His reply was: 'It's all right, sir. I've just finished.'

Those were the last words I heard him speak. That night, at home, he had a heart attack, rolled out of bed, and died at once. He had been our friend for twenty-five years.

PART THREE
Old Residents

ONE

Cricket

THERE CAN be no doubt that the loss of that dear fellow affected our lives as countryfolk more seriously than any other event. It might be said that we were never afterwards as carefree as we had been before. A prop had fallen. He had, of course, a successor; a sensitive man who, although a willing worker, sometimes passed into dream, thereby underlining the patiently methodical ways of our prop. We were very fond of him, as we still are; but he had not been trained as a gardener; he had been seriously gassed on the Western Front as a young man; his occasional abruptness of manner and summary resistance to anything like peremptoriness had led to misunderstanding with other employers; and he worked well for us because he liked us. In the end, he decided to do other work; so that we were left for a time to tackle a giant problem by ourselves.

We had been spoilt. It was so much our habit to rely on our friend, who when we were away took charge of everything and worked harder than ever, that we missed him all the time. No longer did I receive in absence the letters which told us the very things we wanted to know about our home; no longer, being at home, was I spared all the disagreeable jobs which he would not allow me to do; no longer was my hedge-clipping a sort of privileged indulgence, to be undertaken when I felt the need of a little activity in the open air, and to be left for another to finish when I was forced to be indoors. I was reminded that 'life is real, and life is earnest'; and the full size and complexity of the cultivation of a large garden loomed terrifyingly upon whatever I have in place of the normal conscience.

I had always known that, like other men, he had his blind spots. Who is without them? He and I shared many tastes, from pipe-smoking to imperfect enthusiasm for Elgar's music; but we never saw eye to eye in our definition of colours, and it must be admitted that his preference among flowers was for the gaudier blooms. And the worst of his blind spots concerned the game of Cricket. He thought the playing of it a waste of time, and the noise running fieldsmen made with their feet as they slowed in overtaking a ball a species of showing off.

To me, this was obscurantism. From the age of twelve, when through some chance I went by myself to Lord's to watch the then celebrated Gentlemen and Players match, I have been a cricket enthusiast. I was never a good player; my lack of muscular strength would alone have forbidden that. But on this wonderful occasion I saw giants of the game, and in seeing them I entered an earthly Paradise.

I sat, unluckily, next to a gross toper who, already full of beer before the match began, swigged at a great bottle while play was in progress, and shouted remarks which he believed to be stentorian wit for the entertainment of those whose ears he could reach. His ridicule was turned upon myself and my clothes, which were home-made and shabby; and all I remember of it was that I was filled with embarrassment. One effort, however, deserves record. When W. G. Grace (who was massive) and A. E. Stoddart (rather meagre in build) appeared together in the pavilion doorway to open the Gentlemen's innings, the wretch bawled, to the tune of a popular song:

'I put my money on the big fat man;
Doo-dah, doo-dah, day!'

Grace made forty-two that morning, to the bowling of
Richardson and Lockwood, and Stoddart twenty-one; so he
was justified. They were followed by A. C. Maclaren, J. A.
Dixon (of Notts), J. R. Mason (of Kent), S. M. J. Woods, and
Gilbert Jessop, all brilliant stars who continue to shine in
cricket history. And, unless I am persuading myself of something I do not really remember, both Grace and Jessop wore
the bright red and yellow striped cap of the M.C.C. Jessop
certainly did so. The final thrill of the day was that towards the
end of it, when the Players' innings was opened by Abel and
Hayward, they faced the bowling of one reputed to be the
fastest in the world, C. J. Kortright. Some years ago Kortright,
as a very old man, was asked by a journalist saturated in the
modern terms of sophistication to describe his 'method'. His
simple reply was: 'I had no "method". I just bowled at the
stumps as fast as I could.'

All these names will mean nothing to those who are not
cricket enthusiasts themselves; but the enumeration of them
will show why I was so glad that our cottage overlooked the
cricket field. There might be no Grace, and no Kortright, in the
village team, but that did not matter. The game was the thing;
and the game was to be played in sight of our upstairs windows.

I remember Walter de la Mare expressing, in conversation,
a fondness for village cricket of the crudest kind. He seemed to
be in love with the notion of the blacksmith leaving his forge
and advancing to the pitch with dangling braces to smite the
ball vigorously into Passen's ga-arden. This was never my ideal.
I like the white flannels and the well-placed field; and a considerable degree of skill in the batsman. I do not much mind the
scoring rate, as long as the fielding is keen and the strikers know
where and how to place the ball for their own and their side's
advantage. The stroke I crave for is the very late cut, when the
ball, by a turn of the wrists, is sent skimming along the ground

behind the wicket so fast that no man in the world can over-
take it.

Ranjitsinhji was a master of this stroke in reverse, as it were,
on the leg side; and I can still see the flutter of his silk shirt as
he executed this 'glide' as it was called; but I still prefer the
late cut. Batting, for me, should be so perfectly timed that
from the ringside only the result of exquisite art should be seen.
The 'cow shot', or 'rustic stroke', as superfine commentators
call it, is only admirable in fading daylight, when a last twenty
or thirty runs are needed for victory. Then, indeed, the luck of
the bold is glorious; then, indeed, the would-be artistic fiddling
of tail-enders who will take no risks is an abomination.

Although Test Matches draw the crowds, and although in
England the excitement of great bunches of West Indians adds
colour to the general applause, I prefer a good, well-fought
club match to a gladiatorial display. At its best, the club match,
or the keen county match (with its even higher degree of skill)
has something of the intricate charm of chess. The fall of a
single wicket may change the fortunes of the day; the defiant
stand of two men who refuse to be intimidated by a close field;
the gradual overtaking of the opponents' score—by singles, it
may be—when time is running short: these are the delights of
an incomparable game.

We have seen many such struggles from our window. We
have also seen them on county grounds within a comparatively
brief car journey. I remember one match at Hove where the
last Sussex batsman hit mightily, and almost scored the six
which would have given his side the victory. Unfortunately for
Sussex, Peter Cranmer, playing for Warwickshire, ran like the
wind, and, amid groans and cheers, caught the ball one-handed
before it cleared the boundary, thus winning the game for his
own team. That was one of the most absorbing matches I have
ever seen.

My dream game would always have been one between Sussex
and Kent county sides, preferably at Hove. Sussex, because

their fielding is by tradition of the highest class (Fender once wrote that it was better than Yorkshire's; and Hobbs, when asked if he expected to score his hundredth century against them, replied candidly: 'I don't know; Sussex are a very hot lot') would have been in the field. Batting, I should have wished for Frank Woolley in form at one end, and Kent wickets falling steadily at the other. If Walter Hammond, for just once, could have been co-opted to bowl for Sussex, I should once more have rejoiced in his beautiful action; but Sussex without Hammond would have satisfied me.

I saw Hammond play his greatest innings against Australia at Lord's in 1938; and nothing could have been finer than that. England had lost three wickets—those of Barnett, Hutton, and Compton, when he strode grimly from the pavilion, growing in size at every step, until he seemed to be a giant. He made two hundred runs that day, with the heroic Paynter, who made a century, putting our hearts in our mouths by cheekily dashing down the pitch for impossible singles, and having to be sent back. And yet I always liked better to see Hammond bowl. An old cricketing enthusiast, agreeing with this, said that his action was the nearest thing he knew to that of his idol, George Lohmann, whom I never saw.

Hammond, as far as I know, had no chance to bat or bowl on our Common, which as far as secular affairs are concerned is the centre of the village. All are free at any time to walk across it. Children play, dogs meet their friends, old ladies, even while matches are in progress, exercise their right to use it as a short-cut to the shops. When that happens, play is suspended; the solitary little figures are amusedly watched until they reach safety; freedom, or 'Commoner's Right', has been once more vindicated.

Shortly after we arrived here, the oldest doctor said to me: 'Cricket is dead in this village.' He has been proved wrong. No political differences and no enthusiasm for 'the telly' has affected what subsequently proved to be a lasting revival. On Saturday and Sunday afternoons we combat sides from elsewhere; almost every evening young men, youths, or small boys have stumps pitched, white-coated umpires at their posts and the scoreboard in action. Cricket dead? Rubbish! We believe that if the Russians took up the game, among themselves, as we play it, Europe would become civilised.

The change from death to abundant life began in wartime, when troops were stationed hereabouts. Canadians brought their baseball matches to our Common and played among themselves; but with us baseball did not prosper. Nor, after the war, did the speedway racing of little boys. Cricket, once lamentably described to me by an American girl as 'a very pretty pastime, but not a national sport', proved the true key to comradeship. When, by force of circumstances, after strong Nonconformist opposition, the game began to be played here on Sundays, that was demonstrated.

The strength of the game continues to come directly from the village players themselves. They include at present all conditions of men, not Walter de la Mare's blacksmith of legend and sentiment, but solicitors, plumbers, chemists, gardeners, electricians, schoolmasters, butchers, bakers, and shop assistants. There is no class distinction. Some have been to Public Schools and some to Elementary Schools; it makes no difference. They are friends who play the game because they love it; and in this generosity of spirit they are a rebuke to the sectionalists among whom I earn my living as a writer.

Now 1956 had a particular meaning for our Cricket Club, which was then a century old. Twelve months before, the Committee began to make noble and elaborate plans to celebrate this event. The plans were carried out with tremendous success. Such pride and generosity were shown in response to them as would astonish a cricket-innocent stranger. Indeed, it seemed as if every member of our Club, every member's wife, every shopkeeper, every boy in the village was determined to help. All, to the number of hundreds, helped.

They adorned the old pavilion, externally with a fine new

clock which was to remind batsmen of the flight of time, internally with new paint and new strip lighting. New seats round the Common were made and old ones repaired. Local nurserymen gave and planted splendid collections of flowers in front of the pavilion. New deck chairs in the brightest possible colours were bought. A well-produced centenary handbook, which took months of labour and research, recorded the Club's history. To all these activities the youngest as well as the most responsible members gave evenings and weekends of co-operation. And, most thrilling of all, the Centenary Match was played.

That was the greatest day the village has ever known. It caused the purest local happiness I have seen since the lights were lit for peace, and it was a success beyond every dream. Five thousand people sat or stood round the cricket field—men, women, boys and girls. Behind them were ranged innumerable cars, which by mid-afternoon were gathered in every direction.

The first of them arrived at half-past seven in the morning. Fair weather greeted the day and two or three brief fits of drizzle were ignored. The atmosphere was that of holiday; the excitement as keen as that of a Test Match, with this difference, that everybody present, crowd and players alike, cared for the game alone.

The principal hero of this celebration, I am bound to testify, was the *Daily Telegraph*'s cricket correspondent, E. W. Swanton, who captained the visitors. It was he who, having associations with the village, had promised many months earlier to pit a worthy team against our own; and the men he brought would have adorned a national side. They included three England players, led by the great Len Hutton; and the rest were all representatives of their counties. Better still, they came as friends.

Nor was our own team disgraced. Its members bowled and fielded grandly and when their turn came to bat they modestly (but unawed) defied some of the very best bowling in the country, including that of Frank Tyson. When one of our boys, at the end of the game, thanked a visiting star for coming many miles to play his part, the star replied: 'I don't think you ought to thank me. I think I ought to thank you for giving me such a lovely day!'

So, when all were full of honour, little boys rushed for autographs, and sometimes received them. A group photograph was taken. The village band played. The cricketers and most of the crowd, well pleased, slowly departed. The ground was clear; the festival over.

Then came the sequel, which is also, I think, significant. The litter was exposed. It was appalling. It did appal. But next morning our groundsman, who coached the youngest cricketers of all, went to the village school and summoned his small enthusiasts. 'Look here, boys,' said he, 'we shan't be able to have our practice this evening unless the rubbish is cleared.' 'That's all right, sir!' shouted the boys. It was all right. Twenty-two boys appeared at six o'clock that evening. By a quarter to seven they had picked up every carton, scrap of paper, and half-burned match; and a game was in progress. The Common was as good as ever.

TWO

Councils

THE PRECEDING chapter may have suggested—as indeed all the preceding chapters have done—that our village is without governance. This is not the case. It has a Parish Council, elected by the votes of all residents; and it has a Clerk to the Council whose interest in all that concerns local affairs is so conscientious that I hesitate to commend him as I should like to do. If I were to enumerate his virtues in public, as I do in private, he would be besieged by the villagers who want this or that instantly to be done on their behalf. He is already overworked. His telephone bell rings at all times of the day; and when not engaged in answering it or preparing memoranda for discussion by the Council he is to be seen driving about in what I think of as a brake in total unconcern with his own health.

He reproaches me with using excessive speed in my own motoring to and from the village, pretending that when on my tail he cannot keep up with me. This exaggeration is a part of his humour and good humour. Though two sizes larger than myself, he has enough physical resemblance to deceive a very casual glance, with the result that I am sometimes asked by newcomers if I have found accommodation for their relatives, or have taken steps to have some necessary repair made to their homes. When, in turn, I complain to him about this molestation he blandly thanks me for taking some of the burdens of Clerkship off his shoulders. This will show that we are on excellent terms. I think him wonderful; he retorts by holding me up as a model for juniors to follow. The resemblance between us lies solely in the facts that we have small white beards and rosy cheeks.

The Council is composed of admirable, time-giving men who meet to discuss village affairs and are then over-ruled by a superior Council meeting ten miles away. This superior Council, I infer, is in turn over-ruled by a County Council meeting a further twenty miles away; and the County Council can always be invoked as the over-riding authority when larger issues are involved. I suppose this is what is called democratic government.

When something has been done which they do not approve, residents in the village have been known to hold protest meetings in the Village Hall, where the more militant among them are ruled out of order by the Chairman; and I have heard the Chairman's ruling challenged as being out of order. These details will show that the meetings, rare enough, are lively affairs. Tempers are rarely lost. The meetings themselves, in my experience, are usually held after the fact, when it is too late to change anything; and if they have any value it is probably as safety valves. They do not affect friendly personal relations between protesters and members of the Council.

What does the Council do? I have never been a member; and my experience of other committees leads me to believe that individuals have little influence upon corporate decisions. I know that, subject to the superior Authority, our Council tries hard to preserve general equanimity. It has surprised me to find how strong feelings can be, and what things most vex the inhabitants of a village. They range from Common Rights, refuse collection, uneven pavements with consequent puddles after rain (these are a pet annoyance of my own), to litter and noisy motor-cycles. Especially do they concern the interference in village affairs of the superior Councils.

I had, long ago, some trouble with our immediately superior Council. It was not my own affair; but I was appealed to by the neighbour who owned the cows and bees to speak up on his behalf. He had been roughly treated. His home was being flooded because a culvert on the Common was too small. He had apparently asked for it to be enlarged, in vain. I wrote. I received a reply saying, on the authority of an important person, that the culvert had been enlarged, and wrote again, promising that if the important person cared to call I would show him that the culvert was exactly the same size as before. Fortunately I had seen the local Surveyor, who attended with his plans; but the important person did not wait to see the plans. He strode menacingly up to me—he was not only important; he was physically big—and without preamble threatened to give me the rough side of his tongue.

Now, although extremely gentle in act as well as speech, I have never been docile, and am not easily intimidated; so I invited him to let me hear the rough side of his tongue, to which I should retort appropriately. Our gardener, who knew me only as an agreeable customer, was astounded. So was the big man. When shown, by the plans, that he had mistakenly enlarged another culvert, on the opposite side of the Common, he was disconcerted. Casting about in his mind for a way of retreat, he pretended that any enlargement of my neighbour's culvert was a matter for the County Council; but, finding no escape, he submitted. The culvert was enlarged next day.

I subsequently learned the cause of his rudeness. It was that my letter had been read aloud at the superior Council's meeting, where its wit had provoked a roar of shaming laughter. The man is dead. I forgive him. But I still think his attempt to bully me was the result of something I detest in all men—self-importance;—and I cannot really feel penitent for having caused him to be laughed at.

After all, we are ratepayers; and we all share responsibility for the election of candidates for our suffrage. We have a right to be heard, and to express our views without fear. If those we elect have any standing, it is because of our votes. The fact that they are unpaid may give them privileges; they are not to be our masters.

This is well understood in a village; and in this village elections, held in the Primary School, are as informal as can be. When we go to cast our votes, we are liable to be addressed familiarly by fellow-voters and sometimes by those who check our claims by a printed list. Out of doors one of the friendly policemen whom we know by name stands ready to quell incredible rioting. We pause a moment to ask after his health, and perhaps tease him about the easy nature of his duties. Then we depart, hoping for the best.

As we go, we see elderly ladies being helped from their cars as they struggle into the polling station to register their votes for, I am quite sure, the Conservative candidates. The more mobile villagers arrive without assistance, and put their crosses where they please. The names they approve are usually the same as those they voted for last time; and when results are declared the Clerk comments that this shows endorsement of whatever the Council has been doing. I think the Clerk may be wrong. The truth is that there is no scramble for places on any body. I find, in particular, that Secretaries accept their distinction rather ruefully; and only after election does a Chairman or President feel pride at receiving the support of his fellows.

And so, after an Election, matters go on as before. A new Councillor is at first diffident. An old one, who knows the ropes, takes his place with complacency. There is a rustle of papers. The minutes are read. An hour, or two hours, can be passed without deep concern. And in the village matters settle. There has been no great excitement; at the Parish meetings 'the floor', as it seems to be called, may listen but cannot interrupt; some Councillors, more energetic than the rest, will arrange to be available for complaints or inquiries; there is general peace until something is done which stirs a small community to protest; and on the whole we accept with little demur the decisions made, it is said, for our good. Of course we are all agreed that the rates are too high. They, like taxes, are too high everywhere.

THREE

Gardens

FORTUNATELY, WE still have our homes, and our gardens. I once heard two ladies in a shop speaking very urgently. One said: 'I shan't do it!' The other answered: 'Nor shall I!' I expostulated: 'What! Do I hear cries of revolt? Rebellion?' The seemingly irate ladies laughed; and one of them explained: 'We were just deciding that this year we won't buy any "annuals" for the garden: it's a waste of money.'

Another villager told me the other day that she was going to make just a small bed in her garden, with a 'vause' in the middle and some wonderful bargain polyanthus all round it, and, at the corners, little clumps of Spring flowers. This was because her late husband had preferred Spring flowers to any others; and she felt he would like her to arrange the bed in this way. She referred to her husband throughout as 'he', which seemed to me both pathetic and charming.

Gardening, indeed, is a preoccupation with us all. I now understand why one sees, on market days, husbands and wives returning home in triumph with plants they have just bought. I understand why the village is surrounded with many nurseries, large and miniature, with much glass or no glass, all of which are busy from day to day in supplying the needs of eager customers. And since we were given a little plant called picka-back or piggyback on which every leaf grows three, four, or five tiny offspring I have understood why cottage windows are always full of little pots, and why the owners of these pots pore over them so innocently and devotedly each morning.

I also remember how, during the war, as I left London after an air raid which had caused great damage to flats near a great railway terminus, I saw from the carriage window a very old woman, at an upper floor which had escaped destruction, care-fully watering the contents of a window-box. She must have had a shattering night; but she was determined that her ragged little blooms should not go untended. It was probably the same in all bombed cities; it is certainly the same throughout Southern England. Truly 'the purest of humane pleasures' evokes the protective instinct usually attributed to mothers alone!

In what may be called unregenerate, or irresponsible, days, I gaily wrote an article entitled 'Why Gardeners are Gloomy'. It was illustrated on its magazine publication by William Heath Robinson, who saw the theme with equal irresponsibility, and I once saw an advertisement for it in an American publication as 'Swinnerton: Why Gardens Bloom', a very different thing. In that article I enumerated some of the gardener's trials, and described the miseries of men who saw their best endeavours brought to ruin by inclement weather, unseen insects, or un-predictable blight. I added the notification that flowers grew best in places where they had no business to be, such as veget-able beds, gravelled paths, and woodsheds; while the carefully nurtured specimens came to nothing.

Several unknown correspondents wrote ruefully confirming the truths contained in the article, one beginning his or her letter with the statement 'I am the gloomy gardener.' The writer did not seem to be particularly gloomy; and it was clear to me then that no discouragement has ever led to a total abandonment of the craft. Gardeners are always 'baffled, to fight better'.

In 1926 my article was reprinted in a volume called *Tokefield Papers*. I have just re-read it, making the discovery that memory has rosified the state of the garden in our early years of residence. There were *not* always immense crops of apples, and a fine pear tree had been almost killed by a boring beetle (it is interesting to note that when the damage was investigated we found the sinner dead and partly eaten by a centipede, one of those brown wrigglers whose presence in the last dust of a coalshed has always puzzled me). One part of the garden, previously untilled, was infested by slugs. Coltsfoot threatened the strawberries; and the rosebeds were infested with a species of convolvulus. When I praised some particularly fine anchusa I found that they were self-sown, while the legitimate crops had turned sickly and died young. I was correct, however, in one particular: I had grasped the truth that the gloom of gardeners had one prime cause—a knowledge of what the garden *ought* to be like.

This is a philosophical truth, which can be extended far beyond the limits of any struggling acre or two of soil. It applies to the statesman, the painter, the composer, and—let me for once announce a bitter fact—the novelist. All start with high hopes. They sow their seeds or plan their improvements of the human lot, prepare their canvases or exult in their original inventions, as if there were no such things as high winds or resistant populaces, refractory colours or *dramatis personae* who either expand or contract against the writer's will.

Airmen used to call the malign forces 'gremlins'. These were the little devils who crept into machinery or upset calculations to the discomfiture of navigators. They were the evil-doers who beset virtuous persons in medieval fairy tales. They are the personifications of mishap. And all who seek to do anything constructive or inventive are subject to their caprice. In other words, we cannot control our own products, which are affected by climate, health, circumstance, and personal inadequacy. In the garden we plant seeds and hope they will come up as beautiful plants; in the arts we have concepts which we hope will make mighty growths. They almost invariably disappoint us. Neville Cardus reports that the composer Vaughan Williams, after listening to the rehearsal of an ambitious symphony of his own, exclaimed in disgust: 'If *that's* your modern music, you can *have* it!'

In the same way the novelist, who cannot hear or focus his work while it is in progress, meets it for the first time as a whole in proof. Being far more sensitive to a failure in performance than the normal skipping reviewer can be (the reviewer being unaware of original design and months of emotional strain), he looks aghast at the finished work. The symphony, the rose garden, the expert structure of design has gone. He knows what his book should have been like; when what Stevenson called 'the heat of composition' has subsided, he is left with a shrivelled carcase. This is what makes him impatient with superficial criticism; his own deeper dissatisfaction is beyond the range of summary judgment.

He and the gardener are at one. Strangers, visiting a garden, see a profusion of flowers, well-or-ill arranged. The gardener sees only the weeds, the rusty leaves, the consequences of assault by slugs or wireworm. The author sees one more missed opportunity, the result of adverse winds, interruptions, brief ailments, and, within all, failure of talent or its cultivation. I could write quite a good article on 'Why Novelists are Gloomy'.

If there were no compensations, both gardeners and novelists would cut their throats or take to road-sweeping. Let us forget the novelists, and concentrate on the gardener. If he is an amateur, as my wife and I were amateurs (I use the word in this instance as it is commonly understood, as the plural of 'ignoramus', and not of 'connoisseur') he will have two primary

143

indignations. First comes the seedsman's packet, or catalogue, where every flower and clump of flowers is brilliant with growth; and second comes the professional gardener's advice to the tyro. 'Do this, do that,' says the expert; 'prune to the outward bud,' 'plant in a well-shaded spot,' 'do not over-water,' 'the shoots should be . . .', etc. He takes it for granted that the time and the place and the loved plant will be all together. No hint is given that outside buds may not be discoverable, nor that there may be snow in May, nor that some shocking malformation may have occurred in the preceding weeks. He is a man of theory, whose plants always do as they are told to do; a man who, in his heart, despises the ignoramus.

'Show me! Show me!' sings the heroine of *My Fair Lady*. She has taken the words from the lips of the stumbling learner. It was a fault of our priceless friend that he wanted to do all the gardening himself, and had no time to take pupils.

I shall never be more than a spare-moment gardener. For a naturally indolent man I work very hard at my own craft and almost equally hard in an effort to keep pace with a multifarious correspondence. I can see something ought to be done. I plan to do it. I hurry indoors for the secateurs, or in search of a spade, saw, clippers, or fork; and am on the point of executing a noble mission when I am called to the telephone, or remember that I must positively write a letter to the other side of the world or look up a reference for a promised article or the book I am writing. The tools are laid down, or the job is half-done; and when I pass that way again I am irritated by a sense of incapacity. I look at the weeds, many of which, if only they were rare, would be botanically cherished, and compare myself to a horrible old man I once knew who had two particularly bad habits. One was to let every weed in his garden choke the flowers he planted; the other was to tear whole books to pieces in order to extra-illustrate the bulging few of his choice. I am filled with temporary self-loathing.

Meanwhile, the weeds prosper; and if it were not for the

helpful birds, from woodpeckers to sparrows and industrious starlings, the garden might degenerate into partial wilderness. Seeds from the nettles and thistles would spread far and wide, across hedges into other gardens; and no sporadic slashing and uprooting would prevent a return to the forest primeval. We saw what happened among the bombed sites of the city of London, which were quickly crowded with willow-herb and other weeds from afar. The same thing could happen at home. What was so picturesque among the rubble would be much less welcome in cultivated soil.

You could say that the possibility represents the seamy side of 'the purest of humane pleasures.' I do not agree. As a gardener, I know that masses of cow parsley should be ruthlessly cut down, and that dandelions are a pest of the first order; but as a man with an eye to beauty I find the wealth and grace of the first extraordinarily delightful, and the gold and too rapid puffballs of the second among the miracles of Nature.

Let me add a short story on this point. Knowing that my wife's favourite flowers are the daffodils, I bought a large number of these bulbs before we were married, so that on our return from our honeymoon she should have a happy surprise. This came to pass. The daffodils were in bloom in great clumps around apple trees in the orchard. They have bloomed and multiplied in profusion for the best part of half a century; and this year are finer than ever.

Not only is that the case; but in odd corners of the garden, and in uncultivated ground beyond the garden limits, there are smaller colonies, self-distributed, of heroic flowers, 'coming before the swallow dares, and taking the winds of March with beauty.' Whether the March winds or, once again, the ever-active birds, carry miniature corms to a distance, I cannot tell; but the flowers are there for all to see, and the effect is magical.

With us, the same thing happens with the agrostemma, evening primrose, and Michaelmas daisy, so that our rough land is adorned with these flowers, as well as dog roses, milk-maids, blackberries, and, of course, the everlasting nettle. All is Nature; and so it is that Nature compensates for the failures of human contrivance, and makes sure that in spite of bad seasons and bad husbandry the earth produces, day by day, its perpetual surprises. Many of these are the cause of human happiness; some suggest that the old lady does not always know where to stop.

FOUR

Happiness

I WRITE AS a happy man. The admission will at once cause me to be dismissed as trivial by those who pride themselves upon spiritual and intellectual travail; and I shall not be resentful of the contempt. It is a penalty, often paid, for candour. The truth is that I am what is called an extrovert, a person more interested in others than in himself. I have no sense of sin, no vainglory, no troubled consciousness of inferiority to others, and no wish to inflict any dogmatic creed upon the world. In a sense, as I am sure the scornful will proclaim, I have no right to be alive.

Thomas Gray, who described his natural melancholy as, rather, 'a lcucocholy', said that 'to be occupied is to be happy'; and while Arnold Bennett thought me idle it was only by comparison with his own fatal industry, and I have always been fully occupied. I suggest that Gray really was idle, in the matter of poetical composition. He was a busy reader of the Classics, and he longed to be for ever reading the romances of Crebillon and Marivaux. But he shrank from the labour of writing poetry, chiefly, I think, because he had very little of his own to say. This often happens with the learned. Dr Johnson, with the plain man's contempt for dilettanti, said that Gray was dull. What misreadings and misrepresentations of temperament the literary world sponsors!

Bennett's restlessness for work was a disease, not a cause of happiness. He was a victim of the Victorian sense of duty; and was nothing like the tradesman of conventional snob opinion. Nor did he at all resemble the grossly opulent figure of David Low's malicious caricature, on which the envious have built their disgraceful stories of a money-loving vulgarian. Instead, he was a man of exceptional taste and integrity, who felt himself born to protect, even support, all who were weaker or poorer than himself. To me, at our first acquaintance, he was like a keen-eyed father. Then, being very simple, he developed inexplicable respect for an obstinate individuality. He found my naturally cheerful unimpressibility a tonic; and as, owing to his stammer, he was often condemned to silence, he valued the true but irreverent friendship of one who held views similar to his own and who had never in his life stammered. Ours was a very good, entirely unsentimental, friendship, based upon common shrewdness and inability to feel moral indignation.

Bennett was a stoic. He read all the unfavourable and often spiteful reviews of his work as a matter of self-discipline; and of one of them I heard him mutter: 'That . . . is awfully able.' No higher compliment could have been paid.

But, although a stoic, he enjoyed a mental effervescence that led to such nonsensical 'frolics' or 'fantasies' as *The Card* and *Buried Alive*, or, among plays, *The Title* (suggested by his own refusal of a knighthood). The spontaneity of these minor works is disregarded by the priggish, who cannot understand that in some natures the serious and the comic genius co-exist and inter-act.

I have never been a serious person; and have always released my effervescence in conversation, where it sometimes amuses before it bores. Bennett could only do this in company he trusted. The malicious he did not trust. Once, when I complained that another man, expecting a party of bores, had

148

expressly asked me to dinner as a leaven, he laughed and said: 'That reminds me; can you dine on Friday?' I exclaimed with mock indignation. He then said: 'When I have . . . somebody coming that I'm . . . not sure of, I like to have you there.' He meant, as a reliable ally with a ready tongue, who could not be discountenanced. The admission, I still think, was very illuminating of Bennett's character, which, under the stoicism and public self-assurance, had all the sensitiveness of true genius.

I explain happiness, not as Gray did, by busyness, but by temperament and physical condition. Gray was lethargic, and for the greater part of his life a sick man. Although he lived to be fifty-four, he was often so unwell, and sometimes in such pain from a morbid kidney condition, that assidious work was impossible. Also, the very fact that he was an Etonian reminded him that he was socially less exalted than his friend Horace Walpole, the Prime Minister's son and a traveller of constant whim. Hence the early quarrel and, as it seems to me, unassuaged bitterness through life. Gray was not, and could never have been, a happy man.

The happy man is he who has no need to ponder his ill-health or his ill-fortune. If he can eat well, drink in moderation with relish, and sleep quiet o' nights, his health is not troublesome, and he can look about him with lively interest. If his gifts at birth, like those of Shaw's young dentist, include lightness of heart, it would be curmudgeonly of him not to be happy.

From time to time I see in estimates of current literature a figure of speech, taken, I suppose, from gunnery, which charges a writer with 'lowering his sights', or refers to the fact that he keeps them high. As a figure, it seems to me to be a cliché suggesting that all who are not engaged in shooting down the stars are compromising with principle. This is to take Hazlitt's line against Wordsworth, which was that having welcomed the French Revolution in youth Wordsworth retired to the Lakes and sold stamps for an anti-Radical government. It does not apply to those writers who, instead of engaging in politics and self-glorification, tend to look more quietly around them and describe what they see. This may be a personal vanity, because I was once told by a first-class oculist: 'You have an extraordinary range of vision.' Since I would rather see far and wide than into the abstract, I naturally applied the words to more than my eyesight. I remembered that one of my favourite authors, Jane Austen, who also had a light heart, took little interest in the abstract.

Some men, many men, are otherwise constituted. They are driven by demons within to destroy ('Would we not shatter it to bits?'), or to instruct, exhort, or control. They need vehement faith or violent action. Indignant at wrongs, usually to themselves, they are in constant flame; and, since all who are not with them are assumed to be against them, insults are always on their lips or the ends of their pens. Carlyle was, on paper, a very angry man. I had a friend of similar fury, who in youth was all for a religious crusade, and, as time went on, for Communism, and finally for an economic creed called Social Credit. When I sent him a very temperate study of Social Credit, he replied: 'I shan't read it. Anything said against Social Credit makes me unbearably angry.'

Another kind of man has a sense of innate superiority to his fellows. He walks through life with his head in the air, like Samuel Pepys's neighbour, who 'made as if talking to somebody on horseback'. He cares only for the first class in any *genre*, and is scathing in condemnation of little groundlings, who apparently have no sights to lower. One man of this type could admire only what nobody else had ever heard of. When he found that I also admired a novelist who was his latest enthusiasm that unfortunate writer was at once discarded.

The world would be very unexciting if there were no reformers. They sustain the adventure of living. It would be less amusing if there were no intellectual snobs. They have provided authors, from Molière to Aldous Huxley, with endless material for jest. Without fanatics, however, this same world would be more rational, and fuller of loving-kindness, which all philosophers, whatever their lingo, commend. I therefore take my stand with that artful old scholar, Erasmus, who comfortably said: 'We have not all the strength for martyrdom,' and while others fulminated and persecuted went on with his chosen work. At its lightest, wisest, and most original, that work can be read with pleasure more than four hundred years after the death of Erasmus. Could as much be said of Martin Luther's denunciations of Papal fallibility?

I said I wrote as a happy man. I have been as lucky in marriage as in almost all other things. My wife is the ideal companion for a man of my temperament. H. G. Wells, intending a compliment, said 'You feel she's always the same,' meaning that she was a young woman without whims or vagaries; and in this respect he was right. She loves her home, is tender, loyal, and miraculously unselfish. She has also considerable wit, which she says that I alone fully appreciate. She has been so invariably kind a mother that she and our courageous and very attractive daughter have a beautiful mutual understanding; and, without sentimentality, she supports me in fortunately rare moments of discouragement. Her courtesy is superb; her social fault, excessive modesty.

And, finally, we share common amusement in all sorts of nonsense and all sorts of triviality. I am not, as Swift was, obsessed by the littleness of mankind; but, from a frivolousness which I do not defend, find entertainment in the pomposities of academics and the flouncing of too-easily offended great folk. These seem to me to be absurd as instances of human vanity in those who should know better. I deplore and pardon them. And as Elizabeth Bennet earnestly said to Fitzwilliam Darcy:

'I hope I never ridicule what is wise or good. Follies and nonsense, whims and inconsistencies, do divert me, I own, and I laugh at them whenever I can.'

I also laugh at mishaps to myself, at Compton Mackenzie's

never-failing supply of puns, at little boys and girls, at slips of the tongue, the oft-repeated clichés of those who speak on the Radio or Television of 'productivity', 'euphoria', 'challenge', 'exciting', 'basically', or other words which they use for grandeur's sake, and, as the next chapter will show, at the behaviour of those whose vocabularies are limited to expressive barks, miaows, and squeals. All those animals, by my definition, are lovable 'characters', and observation of them has helped to keep me from solemnity and self-importance for the better part of a century.

Arnold Bennett is said to have ejaculated, in looking at an unfinished painting of himself, 'I don't care what anybody says; I am a nice man.' I will not emulate his boast; but instead will say 'I don't care what anybody says of me; I have had a happy, lucky life, for which I am grateful to all who have contributed to it.' There have been many. I salute them.

FIVE

Cats and Dogs

TURNING TO the barkers, miaowers, and squeakers, I shall now, with permission assumed, describe some of these original creatures in more detail. Our cats have been eight in number. Strays have always journeyed to the cottage, as though a path thither had been signposted; and although we have never kept a dog we have not therefore been dogless. Dogs and cats, to say nothing of the guinea-pigs, all appear in a book I wrote for children some twenty years ago, a book (*The Cats and Rosemary*) which has suddenly come to life again in the United States and may be destined to outlive graver writings.

In that book, for purposes of fiction, I assembled all the animals at one time; but not all of them lived simultaneously. The first was a delightful small black cat, very silky-haired, whose tail was a mere bobble. He was brought to us as a kitten from the other end of the village, in a paper bag; and from the moment of his arrival he showed a quickness of thought which was only equalled by his pride. We called him Bogey, because he had only one almost invisible tuft of white on his chest. His paws were tiny, and the pads were black. However far away he might be in the garden, he always caught sight of us and came trotting in our direction with his bobble fluffed out in pleasure. His cracked little voice joined in every conversation; and he often joined me in the studio, standing on his hind legs and rattling the door-handle to gain admittance. Once inside, he curled up on a chair until I was ready to go indoors. Then he trotted beside me. He was specifically my cat, as none of the others have been.

He made it clear to cats from elsewhere that the garden belonged to him; and his chief enemy, whose name was Peter (afterwards changed to Silas by a neighbour who befriended him) was often engaged in combat. Peter, a rather larger cat, learned his place. But Bogey was not naturally aggressive. He was remarkably gentle, and so intelligent that it was a pleasure to watch the movement of his golden eyes as he received impressions or considered plans of action. He did not turn his head, as another very intelligent cat did in thinking of chairs or windows or bedrooms that might be useful, but sat very quietly, eyes moving, ears alert, recognising every step, and fastidiously rejecting food outside his regimen. His fish was whiting; his meat pig's heart. If anything else was offered he would turn from the plate, kicking his hind legs disdainfully. It was to Bogey that I heard my wife one day cry in desperation: 'Well, you'll just have to make do with a little lamb!'

He sometimes brought fieldmice home, and set them free. They, for their part, as if sharing the self-deceptions of the ostrich, went into corners and hid their faces; so that we were forced to pick them up and take them back to their natural haunts. Bogey was no longer interested. Once, when he returned home soaked to the skin with dirty water, after being dried and restored to composure with warm milk, he remembered the indignity he had suffered, stopped drinking, stamped a foot in anger, and gave a sharp sobbing cry of rage, as a boy might have done who had been tumbled into a pond by some lout. Only after much coaxing did he recover his calm.

Alas, Bogey lived for only six years; and after some days of what must have been illness he withdrew silently to die under the front hedge. I found him there and brought him indoors, carrying his light body in my two open hands. As we came up the front path he gave a deep human groan that nearly broke my heart; ten minutes later he was dead.

The very next day two cats who had been befriended by the gardener, who entertained them in his shed with food brought from the kitchen and his own home, waited at the back door for admission. They knew the custodian of the place was no more, and proposed themselves as his successors. They were accepted.

One was a young ginger tom whom we named Brown, the gentlest un-neutered cat I have ever known, who was so much savaged by marauders whom he never attempted to fight that his throat was torn open, and had to be painted daily. This operation was performed by the gardener and myself, and although it must have been very painful Brownie always caressed us both as soon as it was over. He then was left in peace for a few months; but in the end a further assault put him past relief. The other was the redoubtable Daisy Buchanan.

She was a black-and-white stray, who, as an unwanted kitten, followed a cottage neighbour home from a local stable. She tried to live with the neighbour, and then with a lady who provided teas for genteel travellers. With sound instinct, however, she recognised our home as her ideal. During Bogey's lifetime, she had discovered that he used for egress and ingress an ever-open upstairs window (reached by way of a greengage tree), and she stole in that way, slipped downstairs, and raided his saucers. When disturbed she instantly fled; but she returned again and again, with the pertinacity of one who refused to starve in a land of plenty.

Another device was a monkey-like climb up a fine pyrus japonica on the front of the house, which enabled her to enter our bedroom by the window. In the middle of the night her scrambling arrival woke us up in common fright; and again she left in a hurry. In this case, also, she returned, flying as before.

Once established as a resident, she showed that all the craft by which she had sustained herself from kittenhood was merely heightened by prosperity. She fed well, boxed Brownie's ears, and encouraged all the boy cats in the village. And, day by day, she increased her hold upon our affection. Thus her life was that of a Dickensian waif who left poverty behind through quickness of wit, clever adaptation to circumstance, and a seizing of every opportunity for advancement. Poor cat makes good!

She was a natural mother; and when our second daughter was born constituted herself the child's guardian and playmate. She was attentive to everything that happened. The little girl, who inspired trust and affection in all animals, responded. They were constantly together. Buchie would sit as close as possible on the floor, watching contentedly as the child played with her toys, and if these were bricks she entered the game. When the bricks, which were placed one on top of the other, had reached what she considered a sufficient height she would raise a paw and give them a smart pat which brought the structure to ruin.

Of course this intervention evoked protest, to which (for Buchie was the first of our talking cats) she replied with great resource, claiming that she was only giving a helping paw. The game was resumed. Buchie watched as before. By this time she must have been quite mature, although she lived to a great age, possibly seventeen or eighteen years, and she had lost a number of her teeth, so that her speech had taken on some peculiarities; but she was never at a loss for words, always kept her mischievous high spirits, managed to insinuate herself into every photograph in the house or garden, and made a point of escorting all visitors to their cars. She liked to sit on a post outside the front gate, fearlessly chased all strange dogs, and once quite scandalised two passing ladies by smacking first the face and then the rear of their enormous bulldog. She was that attractive being, a character.

She had very sharp claws, and a habit of rolling on her back, inviting a friend to rub or tickle the white stomach. It was a favourite trick. The friend needed to be very alert, however, for 'roly-poly' quickly turned to 'lions and tigers', which involved the use of sharp claws; and as a sequel to 'lions and tigers' came 'all in', in which she went berserk. The friend's hand, purely in fun, would be severely lacerated.

Buchie, although recognising that they must not be chased, kept a sharp eye on two regularly visiting dogs. One of these was a rather nervy, irritable wire-haired fox-terrier named Tinker; the other a splendidly good-humoured Irish terrier named Kim, who, having several times escorted his young mistress to the house, afterwards came to call on his own account, often staying all day.

Buchie also took it upon herself to superintend the lives of the three guinea-pigs, never harming them, but occasionally squeezing into one of the cages, and curling up snugly in the fresh hay. The pigs were not afraid of her; but I think were glad to have their cages to themselves when, hearing a rattle of plates, she decided that something of interest was occurring in the kitchen.

Kim, the Irish terrier, a noble and humorous dog who always rubbed noses with the father guinea-pig, was respectful to Buchie, wagging his tail and looking benignly down upon her. She therefore tolerated him. Tinker, on the contrary, was neurotic, and caused her frequent exasperation. Her occasional cuffs were light, and Tinker did not run away (as she did in panic during an air raid); but I think dislike was mutual, and there were times when Tinker shrank under a merciless glance. She may have noticed, as we did, that although Buchie's nose was usually white as milk, it always became a bright pink when she felt naughty.

Kim belonged to friends whose house overlooked another part of the Common, and whose daughter went to school with ours when both were six years old. When sent out for a walk in the early morning, he hurried round to see us, barking loudly in the front garden. He then visited the kitchen and the guinea-pigs, and if my wife went shopping he accompanied her. Sometimes they lost each other, in which case he would bark outside the shops and even force his way into them. Once reunited, he became as quiet as a mouse. Then he escorted her home, leapt into an armchair, and curled up as if for the next twenty-four hours.

In the evening, always at the same time (knowing, we thought, that his dinner must then be ready) he became restless. He then had to be given what was called his 'present', a bone, or even a piece of bread, which he held in his mouth as he went to the gate. Sometimes the present was not absolutely to his taste, in which case he would drop it in the path, looking round, and wagging his tail; but he was a courteous and appreciative dog, so that he always picked it up again, sighing in resignation, and ambled away in good humour. At eight o'clock next morning his great bark was heard; he had returned for another friendly day.

At one time we were advised that our little girl had what was called a 'grumbling' appendix; and the appendix was removed at the village hospital. We arranged that my wife should visit the invalid in mid-morning and I in mid-afternoon. Kim, of course, escorted my wife, and although a big notice on the hospital door said 'No dogs admitted' he marched straight in and, after a friendly greeting, threw himself down beside the bed. A doctor who was not attending our daughter, but whom we knew as another parent, came into the room on a kindly visit, saw Kim, exclaimed, and launched into a complaint that this brute had killed two of his own dogs. It was a severe charge, made with some flamboyance, and always denied by Kim's owner; but only Kim remained unperturbed. My wife, already aware that he had no business in the room, expressed regret, and explained that Kim was not our dog. Also that he was present only through persistent affection for herself. The doctor, un-

158

appeased, and still complaining, withdrew. Kim remained until it was time to come home.

That same afternoon, as I set out for the hospital, I noticed that the little dog Tinker was following me. Now we had been told by her owner never to take Tinker to the village without a lead, and I had no lead. Therefore I stopped and addressed Tinker. 'You must go back,' said I. 'I'm sorry: but it's forbidden.' Tinker averted her head, with much tail-wagging, and pretended to accept her fate. When I had gone half-way across the path beside the cricket field I found that she was still behind me, although at a greater distance. I again explained, this time more sternly; and she seemed to turn for home. In the end we reached the hospital together.

Tinker, whose great 'line' was humility, stopped and read the notice 'No dogs admitted'. She paused, glanced at me, wriggled, and sat on the step. I paid my visit. On my return, to find her waiting there, she capered gleefully, preparing to depart. As she did so, the same indignant doctor emerged from the hospital. He took one glance at Tinker, and in a loud voice cried: 'Good God! Is that *another* dog that doesn't belong to you?' Convinced that my wife and I were engaged in persecution by means of Snarley-yows, he leapt into his car, and drove off in dudgeon. Tinker and I went home together, Tinker in such high spirits that Buchie smacked her at sight.

We have had other cats since, all of them ginger, or what is courteously called 'red' tabbies; and all have had entirely different temperaments and habits. Furthermore all have particularly attached themselves to different members of the family. Apart from Buchie, also, our cats have avoided the sin of bird-catching. They have occasionally brought home field-mice; but blackbirds have consistently ignored them, with safety. They have all walked over the roof. One, the largest, had two passions; firstly of sitting-in with his mother's later kittens, secondly of trying to cram his great bulk into small boxes or paper bags. When he succeeded in this latter object his mother always pounced on the bag, and split the paper, so that he emerged crestfallen.

His younger brother detested kittens; but had original ways of making sure that, without raising his voice, he was admitted to the house. This boy was once missing for nine days—we think perhaps stolen by somebody who coveted his beautiful coat;—but he returned at mid-day on a Sunday, rattled as usual at the arm of a casement window, ran from one to another of us in crazy delight, visited every room in the house as if satisfying himself that he was really at home again, climbed on to my wife's lap, put his arms round her neck like a baby, and went to sleep.

Not one of these cats was ever a thief. All were fastidiously clean. Each had preferences in the matter of food and sleeping accommodation. Each has defended the house and garden against would-be lodgers. All have demonstrated not only a high degree of affection for the family as a whole but a capacity for thought and sensitive understanding of tones and even words which has been truly remarkable. They have been among the pleasures of our lives.

SIX

Reflections in
a Garden

ONE OF the delights of gardening is that it absorbs the
attention. Time passes very quickly indeed; too quickly,
as life does; and if the work is to be done properly there must
be no carelessness. There is an even deeper delight, which lies
in the concurrent release of memory. Something like 'the stream
of consciousness' is produced in the gardener.

It is vague; it is shot through with memory; and its indulgence, I suppose, increases with age. Having always been a
ruminant, free from the itch to be hammering or hitting a ball,
making a noise or fiddling with machinery ('all good things,
brother'), I dream or ponder like an old woman by the fireside
whose life is over. Unlike the old woman, I use secateurs, a
garden fork, or a pair of clippers, and enjoy the looks and sounds
of Nature. The activity refreshes a spirit that is not yet, as far
as I know, exhausted.

Does one ever know one's own barrenness? Judging from
observation, I think not. My belief is that in every nature, as in
every flower, there is a slow process of growth, a short period of
bloom, and then a decline, sometimes, in the case of a human

being, disguised by a continuance of success, but in the end a weakening of mind or talent which nothing can stay. It is the growth which is interesting. That is shown in the rise and decline of Empires. It is shown equally in the emergence of a politician, his rise to supreme power, his subjection to all the arts of defamation, and his fall. Another proof of an inevitable process lies in our diminished interest in the work of great writers, which, after a time, seem to belong to the day before yesterday. Nothing is more out-of-date than a book we have admired ten or twenty years ago. In literature it is exceptional for any man to continue to produce poetry or prose of superlative originality once he has passed the point of achievement.

This is true of Wordsworth, who in his early maturity was idolised; it was remarked all too soon of Tennyson by his friend FitzGerald, who saw the first lyric genius yield to proficiency. The same phenomenon can be observed in writers more recently dead; and my impression is that of these only Hardy had a wonderful late flowering and acceptance when *The Dynasts* made him suddenly an immortal. Most men, if they could, ought to stop writing or painting or leading their fellows in the very hour of triumph.

Unfortunately few can recognise that hour; and nobody but the unkind commentator ever tells them to shut up. As the unkind commentator has been adverse from the first moment of emergence, his words are unavailing. Writers think it is the unkind reviewer who should shut up. This he cannot do, because, like the writers, he has his living to earn.

What, specifically, do I think about while gardening? My latter end? Certainly not. I hope that I shall die without giving much trouble to anybody, that I shall be cremated, that I shall be forgotten. A few words may be printed in the newspapers, probably saying how many books I wrote; and then there will be silence, as Hamlet foretold, so I do not think farther of my destiny than tomorrow, when there may be a letter from a friend which will carry my imagination into another home. But I do often think of that friend, those friends, men and women I have known, the odd things seen and heard, in the course of a long life, and, latterly, the disadvantage of success in any public career such as that of politics.

I also think of the pains and pleasures of the crafts—the several crafts—to which I have given my days. Gardeners have many plagues, from weather to pests; but they can always pass from one activity to another, and see at a glance the results of what they have been doing. This power is a boon which should be counted at the end of every day. It is recognisable by a writer only when he has performed a relatively small task, such as reading a manuscript, writing a review or short article, or delivering a broadcast. He is able to say, over such brevities, what the wicked lady said in *The House of the Arrow*, 'that will do now'. When the red light goes out in a broadcasting studio, he knows that this particular work is finished. The novelist has no similar comfort.

He is like a man swimming the Channel, sometimes like a man swimming the Atlantic. Having embarked upon a book which is to fill his mind for months, he is at first hopeful that he can execute it with some credit. Within a few days he has left the safety of the shore, and all too soon has lost sight of it altogether. Waves of difficulty sweep over his head. He can stop, as many before him have stopped, and abandon the enterprise altogether; George Gissing once noted in his diary that before beginning *The Odd Woman* he had made six abortive attempts on other books. Driven by determination, Gissing battled on. So does every professional novelist; sure of only one thing. This is that one day the journey must be completed. And he knows that when it is over some bright junior will be writing to dismiss a year's toil in a flippant or contemptuous sentence.

This is very bitter if he is sensitive, as for example H. G. Wells was sensitive. Wells was told, as Shaw was told by dramatic critics, that his efforts were not worth making; that whatever strokes he made were ill-judged; and that he himself was a creature of no worth. Instead of writing an article called 'Why Novelists are Gloomy' I ought to write one on 'Why Authors think themselves the most ill-used of Atlantic Swimmers'.

The calling has great pleasures. One is the continued practise of a difficult craft. A second is that contact is made with all sorts of men and women, most of them un-met, who come to regard the writer as a friend. While gardening, I think what these correspondents have meant to myself. I speculate about them, and fill in the details which they have not mentioned about their personalities. It is a fascinating occupation. Expressions of kindness pop into my head as I squint along a hedge, observe its symmetry, and relish my own artistry; or, while digging, I meet a robin's confident stare before he nips down to secure an excavated treasure. When this happens, I know that he and I, in our several ways, look on life with comparable zest and are masters of our own techniques. The certainty, while it lasts (no longer than two minutes), is ravishing.

Diversity is provided by many strangers who, in all innocence, are writing books or theses upon some modern figures, and ask to be told all I know about these. The inquiries go back to days before I was born, testifying to the fact that my age has become a legend; but even to be asked what I remember of Victorian masters is, in a way, as Smee said of the crocodile's desire for Captain Hook's second arm, 'a sort of compliment'; and when it is paid I am set digging, not only in the garden, but into the medley of past reading, anecdote, and personal contact.

This is what old men are for; to help the young. They are lucky to be given the chance.

Well, then, what do I remember? As I have said in another book, the first literary figure I ever consciously set eyes on was a well-known editor and book-reviewer of the day named Clement Shorter. This was in 1899; and he was struggling across

164

Fleet Street at Temple Bar (which then stood in its historic position at the junction of Fleet Street and the Strand), a stocky figure, very swarthy, wearing black-ribboned *pince-nez*, and carrying under one arm a good half-dozen review copies. The uniqueness of this glimpse of the book world fixed it in my mind for ever.

In the following years I had other glimpses, without acquaintance. I saw Rudyard Kipling outside his house at Rottingdean, Hall Caine, subsequently, with a finger to his forehead, in the balcony at a Queen's Hall Promenade Concert, and George Moore as he solemnly drooped across the stage to his box at the Sunday night performance of an Irish play. I was given a ticket for the Memorial Service to George Meredith in Westminster Abbey, and must have recognised some of the distinguished people present, although the only one I remember is H. H. Asquith.

I never saw Thomas Hardy or Henry James. Friends of mine, Siegfried Sassoon, W. J. Turner, St John Ervine, and H. M. Tomlinson, frequently visited Hardy; I, to my regret, did not. And when Henry James died (he being one of my heroes and 'influences', as they are called) I lamented to Hugh Walpole the fact that I had not seen him. 'Oh, Frank!' exclaimed Walpole. 'Why didn't you tell me? It would have been easy to arrange.' And, after a pause, 'I don't know that you'd have liked him.'

That was not the real point. I have never been one of those who cultivate the famous and cherish the memory of having shaken hands with them. Reverence is not in my line; and there have been many famous people for whom I have had no respect at all. James was in a different category altogether. I had read *The Portrait of a Lady* at the age of twenty-one, with a rapt attention which I have never forgotten. I owned it, and still own it, in the little blue cloth three-volume pocket edition published in 1883, the year before my birth; and for me *A Small Boy* and *Notes of a Son and Brother* constitute one of the most beautiful autobiographies ever written.

For this reason, among others, I should have welcomed a

chance to hear James's rather laboured search, in conversation, for the appropriate word. I should also have liked to verify the truth of William James's description of his brother, which I believe to have been profound. It was:

'Harry has covered himself, like some marine crustacean, with all sorts of material growths, rich sea-weeds and rigid barnacles and things, and lives hidden in the midst of his strange heavy alien manners and customs; but these are all "protective resemblances", under which the same dear, old, good, innocent and at bottom very powerless-feeling Harry remains, caring for little but his writing, and full of dutifulness and affection for all gentle things.'

It may be that I should not have liked him. My old friend Horace Horsnell, who was once Wells's secretary, did not do so. He found James inquisitive. Walpole unquestionably grew out of veneration for the old man, and neglected him, thereby causing a deep wound to that exceeding sensitiveness. Wells, resenting James's criticism, wrote rudely of him in *Boon*. But when, knowing Wells's regard for William James, I made some remark about the brothers, he said quickly: 'Oh, but Henry was much the greater man.' I wish I had met him.

Having said this, I pass to one constant theme of meditation, the fascinating way in which literary generations overlap, and have always overlapped. While historians speak of 'The Elizabethan Age', or 'The Victorian Age', there are, in letters, no such arbitrary divisions. The ages dovetail. The great Edwardians, as they are called, were all born in the reign of Queen Victoria. However much they may have reacted against their immediate forerunners, they settle in time into an unbroken sequence.

Something similar is true also of the men of Regency days, who were all born in the eighteenth century, Wordsworth only ten years after George the Third came to the throne. He was fourteen when Dr Johnson died, as Coleridge was twelve, and Lamb and Jane Austen were eleven. These names are enough

166

to prove how true it is that a marvellous century of change is traduced when it is called 'the age of Reason'.

Speaking impromptu at a public luncheon, I once amused an audience containing many junior authors by mentioning that I had familiarly known E. V. Lucas, editor and biographer of Charles Lamb; and that Lucas, a curious mixture of hardness and sentiment, cherished one mystical joy. While engaged in research for his work, he had met and shaken hands with the widow of Edward FitzGerald, and Mrs FitzGerald, daughter of Lamb's friend, Bernard Barton, had shaken hands with Lamb. To Lucas, the fact of such a succession of handshakes was symbolic. He felt that, at a respectful distance, and, as it were, by proxy, he had touched the hand of his idol.

He had shaken hands with many living men, so that he felt he had passed to them something of the same privilege. He thought less of meetings with Hazlitt's grandson (a silly, pompous little man whose every sentence began 'my grand-father, William Hazlitt') but perhaps the knowledge that, like Lucas himself, Mrs FitzGerald was the member of a Quaker family heightened the sense of communion.

Pursuing the anecdote in my casual remarks, which were a sort of thinking aloud, I pointed out how Lucas's encounter with one who remembered Lamb could be extended back through literary history. Lamb was only nine years old when Johnson died; but his sister Mary was nineteen. She claimed to remember that when her parents lived in the Temple, she, as a little girl, had one day looked out of a window and seen Oliver Goldsmith walking in the garden below. Since Goldsmith died in 1772, when she was about seven, this was possible. Now Thomas Gray, physically a little man, was strolling in London a few years earlier with his friend Bonstetten, when he saw and recognised, not Goldsmith, but Johnson. 'Look, look, Bon-stetten!' he cried. 'The great bear! There goes *Ursa Major!*' He did not address Johnson, whom he did not know; but, as you see, he could recognise him and was aware of Johnson's reputed characteristics. Gray's friend Horace Walpole, more of a snob than Gray, and later one who had his misadventures with Boswell, dismissed both Goldsmith and Johnson as not worth attention, on the ground that 'I have known Gray, and *seen Pope!*'

These glimpses and comments took us back a century. Nor was that all. Walpole, for all his sight of Pope, had not known Pope's friends Addison and Swift; but we know how these two men talked and walked with Vanbrugh and Congreve, and we know that Addison cheered the last ten years of Dryden's life with his gay conversation. In younger days Dryden had applied—in vain—to John Milton for employment under Cromwell's government; and, although adamant with Dryden, Milton did assist Sir William Davenant, who took pride in being, he said, the natural son of Shakespeare. Thus was bridged another century.

I could not, in this connection, go farther back than Shakespeare. For one thing, I knew no more; for another, I did not want to labour a fancy, and I had made the point. But is not this a theme for rumination? I find it so.

Most of us, if we have any curiosity about the past, would like very much to question our seniors about those who were old when they were young. Questions would not be as stupid as that derided by Browning: 'What porridge had John Keats?' They would be 'What were they like?' 'How did they walk, talk, laugh?' 'Is it true that Coleridge always spoke with a West Country accent?' 'Were Herrick and his friends as bucolic as Rose Macaulay made them in *They Were Defeated*?' 'Were Shakespeare and Ben Jonson at the Mermaid really as brilliant in talk as they are reported to have been?'

These are my own curiosities. They arise from the sparseness of information on just these points. We know much more about the looks and ways of certain other famous men; for examples, those references to Swift's azure eyes, height, penuriousness, and 'insolence' to be found in Spence's *Anecdotes*, and the examples of talk between Johnson, Burke, Goldsmith, and Reynolds given by Boswell. We should still wish to know more, especially as Fanny Burney gives some quite brilliant impressions of people like Arthur Young and those, including Johnson, whom she met at Mrs Thrale's or of George the Third, whom she met at Mrs Delany's.

Again, how did Lamb, Coleridge, Hazlitt, Southey, and Wordsworth behave when they met? How did they speak? Carlyle, always malicious about his elders, said that Coleridge roamed about a pathway and snuffled vaguely about 'Ommject' and 'Summject'; Lamb's stammer, like Arnold Bennett's, is a part of literary history; Hazlitt has been described as 'sidling into a room after the manner of a criminal' (which Wordsworth, smarting under criticism, thought he was) but in spite of Haydon's wonderful gift of description they had no Boswell. Even though Caroline Fox excellently tells us what John Sterling said in his conversations with her, giving a direct portrait of him which is far happier than Carlyle's biography, she knew, of the others, only Wordsworth, who remains the least attractive of the group.

It has always been my belief that the one man I have known who could have sat with Lamb and Coleridge in fraternal discourse was Walter de la Mare. I can imagine him asking his fascinating questions and stimulating them to discussions lasting far into the night. When I mentioned my fancy to Pauline Smith, Arnold Bennett's protégée and a writer of beautiful stories about her native South Africa, she said in her reply: 'That is what I have always felt about *you*.' As can be imagined, her words set me longing to have had the privilege. I have not the quality of mind to sustain any sort of debate with Coleridge (I think Walter de la Mare, who was as subtle as he was innocent, might occasionally have stumped him); but ever since, at the age of nineteen, I was initiated by William Macdonald, who edited Lamb, into the corps of fellow-students, I have been fonder of that group than of any other. Its rediscovery of the Elizabethans, and its general approach to literature as unlimited wealth in ideas and language, roused a boy to enthusiasm which has never diminished.

Something more may be said here. When James Northcote was asked, in 1830, how Sir Walter Scott compared as a man with Johnson, Burke, and the rest, he said that, as far as he could judge, Scott 'would have stood his ground in any company'. He added, according to Hazlitt, that the famous men of the previous age 'were not looked upon in their day as they are at present; . . . but because their names have since become established, and as it were sacred, we think they were always so'.

He could not have said this in the nineteen-sixties, which have seen a continuous effort—begun in 1917 by Lytton Strachey—to belittle great men of this and the nineteenth century; but even now, at a level above that of gossip and publicity stunts, there is more interest in the men than in the degree in which they illustrate the vagaries of literary fashion. Tradition obsesses professors, and has importance for students with examinations to pass. It has less importance when we understand the writers themselves and know the circumstances in which they wrote. Then, indeed, we can realise why some made a great noise in life (I think of Carlyle, Ruskin, Herbert Spencer as examples) and are hardly more than whispers to posterity; and why some who made hardly any impression upon their contemporaries are re-appraised and sometimes exalted in the light of fuller personal knowledge.

Take, among more recent authors, two instances. Hall Caine, although Oscar Wilde thought him a ghoul who 'went in with the undertakers', was fantastically praised as a young novelist because he 'discovered' the Manx nation. He became a best-seller because, said his detractors, he dealt in those ever-attractive themes, sex and religion; and—through a frenzied and ribaldly-exploited rivalry in sales of a hundred thousand copies by both *The Christian* and *The Master Christian* with Marie Corelli—ended almost as a figure of fun. Stephen Phillips led a revival in poetic drama at the beginning of the century when he was likened to Shakespeare. He had great publicity and apparent success in the theatre, and perished when the poetic was ousted by newer fashions for the Irish Players, Shaw, Granville Barker, and Galsworthy.

Or take a more interesting case, Henry James. There exists a fretful letter from James to W. D. Howells, written in 1895, in which he says: 'I *have* felt, for a long time past, that I have fallen upon evil days—every sign and symbol of one's being in the least *wanted*, anywhere or by anyone, having so utterly failed. A new generation, that I know not, and mainly prize not, has taken universal possession.' Yet within fifteen years of this cry of despair he was the most impressive literary figure in England. The fashion had veered. He had grown old. The newer generation had lost momentum. By a curious turn, although not much read by the subscribers to circulating libraries, he had become a *personality*. Today, of course, he has achieved even greater fame in the theatre and on Television, where the drama of his stories (as opposed to his plays) is proving ideal material for exploitation. What would he have said? How would he, brimmingly, have found words to express his pride?

I spoke just now of gossip, which in the literary world is usually malicious. The moment a writer attracts attention he is invited into Society. He meets the sets—those whom the publisher, William Heinemann, called 'the little West End clique'; and he becomes known as an individual. This is the beginning of success; for in England any author must be constantly met at dinner- and cocktail-parties if he is to receive the publicity which all too many writers crave.

He then engages the jealousy of his rivals. Stories about him are circulated. If they are amusing, or particularly malicious, they are spread after the manner of the little girls' game of Russian Scandal, half mis-heard, half purposely embroidered. If the author himself, joining in the fray, comments on his rivals in the same spirit, his words are instantly conveyed to the victim or victims. Feuds begin.

171

They begin, whatever happens. Innocent readers may often wonder why they see in the Press a caustic review, or even denunciation of a writer they admire. Or they may wonder at seeing no review at all. They have no means of knowing that in either case the work of retaliation for some affront or imagined affront is in progress.

The attack is not always made by one of the chief actors in the quarrel. There may not have been a quarrel at all. Quite possibly a 'friend' has done the fell deed, out of mistaken loyalty to the other party. One instance of this mischief is the supposed animosity between Dickens and Thackeray. They are alleged to have quarrelled outright over Thackeray's demand for the expulsion from the Garrick Club of an unscrupulous journalist named Edmund Yates, by whom he had been ridiculed. Yates told the story himself. But Mrs Lynn Lynton, who knew both Dickens and Thackeray, denied that there was ever any animus between them. She accused 'friends' (she meant John Forster, who, she said, had already traduced Walter Savage Landor) of inventing and spreading the slander.

I can believe this charge, because I have personally known so many writers of my own generation and the generation immediately senior to it. Within the last few years I have read the story that Arnold Bennett and H. G. Wells were alienated in middle age. It was based on misunderstanding of the fact that they exchanged fewer letters than they had done earlier. The truth was that they wrote less often because both were living in London, meeting several times a week, and talking instead of writing. Their friendship lasted to the end. I myself saw Wells on the morning after Bennett's death. He had been crying.

It is my belief that only small men feel jealousy; the reason being that failure embitters those who have begun with high hopes. The successful can afford to be generous. But the literary world is full of envies; and the envious are easy prey for mischief-makers.

That is the end of another digression; but I hope the digression has been of some interest. It has developed a fancy of my own, has indicated some of the trials which spoil the harmony of what should be a happy calling, and has explained why, having spent half my working life in what has become more and more a struggle for publicity, headlines, high-pressure sales-manship, and film and paperback rights, I am glad to live out of the world, cultivating my garden. It used to be said that Bernard Shaw was a self-advertiser; it is still said that Arnold Bennett was 'commercial'. If either of these charges was ever true, both men have been left far behind.

The truth is that each was cast in his own mould. As the years pass the reputations of both as writers, have had ups and downs; but by degrees they will take their places among the Drydens, Goldsmiths, Coleridges, and Dickenses of former days, carrying on the tradition of English letters and becoming legendary. Indeed, I think they are already legendary, since I am so often invited to tell all I know of them.

I should not dare to make the same claim for those of my own generation. Some are already in limbo; and the rest may well follow. Fashions change more quickly than ever, nowadays, and books go out of print and stay out of print as they were not allowed to do in the past. This greatly assists in the process of oblivion. But the genuine boys and girls will continue to be read in tattered library copies, and it is likely that some of them, too, will become legends. It is an amusing topic for rumination.

SEVEN

Illusions and
Realities

I T MAY be supposed, from the foregoing, that I spend all my
time in a state of happy unreality. That is not so. I dream,
certainly; but I have lived in the hardest of schools, and I still
work a seven-day week, putting away my pen and papers only
at eight o'clock each night. Many young writers, it seems to me,
make the mistake of supposing that once they have published
a book it is their privilege to abandon drudgery and migrate to
the wilds, there to live lives untrammelled by industry, where
genius, idleness and all good things go together.

Sooner or later, they find that the wilds do not produce
inspiration. They produce, on the contrary, little but chilblains
and financial shortage. Expectations of continuing effortless
success are not fulfilled. Wolves come and sit very close to the
door; families begin to need food and clothes, as well as liberty;
and as regular labour becomes more and more irksome the
would-be artists become opportunists. They are driven to apply
for assistance to organisations which are already finding it hard
to help all the cases brought to their notice.

In speaking earlier of St John Adcock I told of such a young writer of an older generation who threw up a good job on the strength of one small literary success, and deteriorated, first into a sponge of liquor, and then into a sponger upon his fellows. He did not migrate from London, because migration from London was then less fashionable than it became later; but he made the mistake I have described.

I did not make that mistake. Not only had I never thought myself a genius, which seems to be a common illusion nowadays; but although I forsook 'the madding crowd's ignoble strife' I retained too much interest in the active world to desert it altogether. Not only the world of books, but the world of men and affairs.

In the nineteen-twenties and thirties, having learned at first hand a great deal about the literary and publishing professions, I knew the dangers of solitude, and spent a part of every week in London. I there consorted with men of note in the journalistic, legal, and political spheres, beginning with the Liberal editors, J. A. Spender, A. G. Gardiner, and H. W. Massingham, with Clifford Sharp of *The New Statesman*. I worked for Massingham and for another Master, J. L. Garvin; and knew the rest, especially Gardiner, a close friend, with considerable intimacy. They all taught me a great deal about business and politics, past and present.

In the same congenial circle were such Liberal M.P.s as Vivian Phillipps, the Liberal Whip; Lief Jones (afterwards Lord Rhayader), and John Tudor Walters; classical scholars such as John Sergeaunt and T. E. Page; the economists J. A. Hobson, Oscar Hobson, and George Paish, and, less regularly, Earl Russell and Lords Salter and Buckmaster. All contributed in their several ways to talk which was the most exhilarating I have known. Though I talked and was listened to, I listened more often than I talked. And the brightest and most constant luminary in this world was a Welshman, formerly an M.P., but then a disengaged, ever-busy man of extraordinary parts named Walter Roch. He left London after the Second War, and dropped from public attention; but he was so exceptional that I should like to add a special word here about him.

Roch was (he died in 1965 at the age of eighty-five) a really astonishing character, so quick that stupid men feared him and were flustered by him. He would briskly join his friends at a particular table in the Reform Club, and afterwards in 'the Corner' in the smoking-room upstairs, where the party swelled from a crowd of ten at a table for six to something like twenty or thirty in what was almost a mass; and as he took his seat he would exclaim 'Well, Arnold,' or 'Geoffrey' or (to myself) 'Swinny', with such gaiety that we immediately guessed he was in the mood to indulge his mischievous gift for teasing or baiting. So sharp was his insight, and so varied and curious his knowledge of politics, the law, and business, that I am sure he could have out-debated any man in the House of Commons but for a single defect of character.

He would put demure questions to his chosen victims, such as Tudor Walters (who was imperturbable), or a solicitor named Geoffrey Russell (who was not); and for good measure would slip in gibes at anybody else who chanced to be present. If these were H. G. Wells or Arnold Bennett, who were as quick as he, the darts were indulgent; but to those less swift he must have seemed like a champion matador.

His fluency, malice and kindness were mingled with social and political gossip, news of the commercial world, and caustic estimates of public men. And as he was 'not only witty in himself but the cause that wit was in other men', the stimulation of his company was glorious. Nor were talk and teasing his only concerns. He read and impatiently (or tolerantly) discussed many new books, and was full of quotations from old ones. He casually admitted that he had played cricket for Harrow and ridden a horse in the Grand National. In middle age he learned at high speed to write a remarkable script; and I remember with amusement a boasting match with Arnold Bennett as to which of them could most efficiently prepare a solicitor's bill of costs. The bill reached a very high figure indeed; and the match was drawn. There was in fact no matter of which he seemed to show ignorance.

I referred to what I thought might be a defect of character. One day, a barrister, later a judge, who had been undergoing trial, protested: 'Look here, Walter, you're always tormenting *us*; but I notice you never attack Swinnerton.' Roch's reply was: 'I'm afraid of him,' and Arnold Bennett commented briefly: 'That . . . is true.' Glances were exchanged around the table.

Now I hope it will not be thought that I repeat this from vainglory: I do so for another reason, which is that I think Roch could have been Prime Minister if he had had the grit fully to use his natural brilliance and command the attention of the House of Commons. He made no impression there. He would not risk his own discomfiture in the virulence of debate. He could be, and was, silenced by harder, tougher, more ambitious men. Therefore he was at his dazzling best in a small appreciative company of men whose foibles he could exploit for the general amusement. He was deterred from attacking me, not as he said, by fear, but by timidity lest he should fail with one whose vanities he could not fathom.

I have spoken of Roch and the others in order to show that retirement to the country need not, and did not in my own case, mean total seclusion. I have always benefited from the friendship of able men; and the reason I now go less frequently to London is that most of my old friends there are gone. The majority are dead; the rest have deserted the town. I forget them while I am engaged in writing; but when able to let thoughts rove without concentration as an undercurrent to outdoor activity I re-live a thousand delights. Then I realise how rich I have formerly been in the company of men who all knew more than I shall ever do.

As a young writer I rejected the approaches of fashionable hostesses; and I did not suffer for my refusals. It was always the company of originals that gave me pleasure. Having known many of them, of every age and size and class, at close quarters,

I still prefer those without a wish to be smart or affected or successful.

Famous men can be, and often are, petty and vindictive. They catch the tone of Society, which is one of insincerity. That is why our villagers, who have no temptation to outwit or outshine their rivals, can bear comparison with the best. They have not learned the defensive cruelties of sophistication.

It is probable that most of the lettered residents in our village have read one or two of my books. It is natural for them to feel curiosity enough to do this, and some, I know, have liked what they read. Indeed, when, three or four years ago, John Baker brought out a new edition of my old book, *Nocturne*, I was told that there was a waiting-list at the local branch library of twenty-six people for the single available copy of the book (on which my royalty was one-and-ninepence ha'penny); and I hope they were all satisfied in time.

My reference to the one-and-ninepence ha'penny was not meant as a reproach. It was a comment on the assumption that all authors are rich. In order to pay for the greatly increased costs of production, publishers have been forced to price the books at a figure which deters private customers. Authors must rely more and more on what the Public Libraries buy; and as, in turn, Public Libraries cannot expand the amounts derived from rate-payers, the shrinkage in authors' incomes is progressive. Many of the older among them, overtaken by ill-health or lessened energy, become poor. Middle-aged authors, without resources, too old to change their profession, and with former expectations dashed, are often in despair. Their wives cannot sleep o'nights; they themselves find invention paralysed; their only hope is of support from the limited income of the Royal Literary Fund.

My knowledge results from many years' membership of the Committee of that Fund. I have no personal complaints. My publishers are generous, and in spite of the fact that I have been publishing books for sixty years I still have loyal readers. But my feeling for less fortunate authors is such that I wish the

British Government would really take in hand the plan which has been drawn up for Public Lending Rights. It would relieve hardship, and give hope to writers who cannot claim, as the Trade Unions can do, incomes proportioned to the cost of living.

I do not expect our villagers to read my books. Some, however, listen to the Radio and watch Television; and to these I am not altogether anonymous. By others I am known only as a familiar face, and among these I include four men who get off their bicycles to chat, and who always talk with great spirit. One is an ex-sergeant of the Inniskillings, another a gardener, the third a coach-driver, and the fourth a man, now retired, who has followed several occupations and studied human nature everywhere. There are others, as well, but these four are rich 'characters'. They keep me laughing for five or ten minutes, and ride off again leaving happy memories.

Having read lately that a Texan literary professor considered English hedges a sign of national decadence (he had evidently not seen the fine stone walls of the less fertile Northern counties) I was at first saddened by suspicion that I had wasted years of effort upon our own. I ought, in his opinion, to have substituted the barbed wire used for divisions in his native State. But if I had done this all the birds which find holly, thorn, and privet ideal resting places would have been driven away. In banishing, at the same time, those self-planted trees which are now converting our small field into a wood, I should have alienated the jackdaws, woodpeckers, and magpies, and the very cuckoo who plots his raids there on the homes of potential foster-parents for his children. Is this thought to be borne? I say 'No!' and 'To Hell—or Texas—with such literary professors of philistinism!'

We have, not Texan professors, but pragmatists of our own. Current fashion in literature and the other arts concentrates upon the abnormal and the disagreeable, current farming upon

179

insecticides and the destruction of those who steal the farmers' crops, current architecture upon featureless height in flats and office buildings where individuals become insects. No wonder that many resisters to these fashions regard the contemporary scene with horror, and suspect human nature of being loathsome. It is the new pessimism.

Pessimism has its warrant. I do not ferociously condemn unimaginative architects, or self-protective farmers, or those who are preoccupied with what, in days of greater sentiment, was called 'the seamy side'. I have had experience of cities, ill-health, sharp practice in trade, great hardship, and treacheries on the part of certain human beings, and I am not a sentimentalist. I sometimes wish, however, that I could skip the next hundred years and look back as a detached historian upon the products of our generation of busy, interfering minds. I should like to know if Hilaire Belloc's prophecy of the Servile State has been fulfilled, and if its consequences, which now appear so destructive of love and amity the world over, have wholly spoiled the countryside and all humane values.

EIGHT

Plea for
Contentment

I DO NOT see how we can escape from the consequences of two wars in which large-scale slaughter was committed. Men argue about the causes of those wars; and they argue very convincingly that the feebleness and incapacity of British leaders were as much to blame as the cynical ferocity of other national leaders. They also demonstrate, as Keynes so brilliantly and prophetically did in *The Economic Consequences of the Peace*, that the Peace following the First World War was bound to produce, as it did, the Second World War. This only means that men in charge of affairs have to decide without profound thought, and under pressure from other determined men, what is to the immediate advantage of their own peoples. They improvise. They make mistakes. They are small, when they should be giants.

Anybody who has even dipped into the history of nations must see that this has always been the case. Because in past ages mistakes were not publicised, we assume that the noted leaders were generally larger than life-size. They have been extolled by poets, and it may be that until, let us say, the reign of Queen Anne, when destructive criticism fell into the hands of such a writer as Swift, or in the reign of George the Second, when Harvey kept his merciless records of the Court, they were able to preserve a dignity impossible to contemporary leaders. As late as the Victorian century free comment could be stifled by the pompous phrase: 'We are too near'. Alexander, Julius Caesar, Burghley, Cromwell, Chatham, Frederick of Prussia, and Napoleon were all 'great'. It is only now that, in accordance with fashion, and by the purposeful ransacking of private records, they are being converted into pigmies.

It is impossible to doubt that past leaders were often bad, quarrelsome men who, if they had been subjected to expert Television interviews and the indignities of paragraph-writers and caricaturists, would have cut much poorer figures. We have no panegyrists nowadays; only critics anxious to belittle.

The Victorian attitude was vividly expressed by Froude, who, as is well known, thought highly of Henry the Eighth. Tempted, as he said, to make a general observation, he proclaimed that: 'Princes, statesmen, thinkers who have played a great part in the direction of human affairs, have been men of superior character, men in whose presence ordinary persons are conscious of inferiority. Their biographers—the writers of history generally—are of commoner metal. They resent, perhaps unconsciously, the sense that they stand on a lower level, and revenge their humiliation when they come to describe great men by attributing to them the motives which influence themselves. . . . They delight to show that the great were not great after all, but were very poor creatures, inferior, when the truth is known about them, to the relater of their actions.'

Being Froude, a man of unexpected turns and inconsistencies, he added: 'I do not wish to say more. You will take my observation for what it is worth.' I shall follow his example, remarking only that the current practice of derision, which makes us all laugh, particularly at its victims, could possibly be criticised in similar terms. I have long wished that writers who psychoanalyse the dead could themselves be psycho-analysed.

As for the satirists and detractors, far too many of them nowadays lead hot-house lives, meeting only those of the same order as themselves in a stuffy atmosphere of malice and ill-nature. The admired are to be held up to scorn; bucolics are to be depicted as boors; only the winkers and nose-pullers are, they hope, safe.

This is a poor sport, encouraged, I sometimes think, by a terror of insignificance. The terror is justified, because the political tendency since Karl Marx has been to emphasise the smallness of the individual and to insist that he must do as he is told by Government decree. Younglings, impatient of authority, throw tantrums; when the lesson of personal impotence is learned they grow fatalistic and riot no more; discouraged, they find their only weapon to be satire.

Satire is not a creative force. Nor is it the only sign of degeneracy. One of today's worst features is the constant effort to show great men of the past as sexual perverts. Lewis Carroll and Kenneth Grahame have not escaped. Jesus Christ himself, it is pointed out, travelled with an all-male band of disciples. And because very sensitive young men, repelled by the ever-bolder behaviour of contemporary young women, prefer to consort with their own sex it is assumed that sodomy is, and always has been, the way of genius.

This arises from the hot-house atmosphere in which too many of those who are disrespectfully called 'highbrows' live. Having known most of the distinguished writers of my own and an older generation, I think we had an easier and more normal outlook. Only four men, from Norman Douglas to James Agate, were believed to be homosexuals. We knew nothing of Maugham's lately-exaggerated abnormality, and, of course, nothing of the fevers revealed in a recent biography of Lytton Strachey and his companions. The fact that so much fuss was made about John Addington Symonds and Oscar Wilde (of whom the former was known to Swinburne as 'Soddington') shows how little it was taken for granted, as it is now, that any friendship between men must have an amorous basis. My own friendships were always untainted; and I think that was true of the majority. But then my friends had not been secluded, in adolescence, or in warfare, from female society; and women were still daughters of Eve.

One word more, and I am done with this subject. We are seeing large numbers of plays and novels in which the authors use, or make their characters use, what are euphemistically called 'four letter words'. I am always reminded, in these cases, of what Rudyard Kipling wrote in *The Phantom Rickshaw* (1888–9) 'When little boys have learned a new bad word they are never happy unless they have chalked it up on a door. And this also is literature.'

Sophisticates are pathetic adolescents, squirrels in a small cage, watching and imitating the antics of other squirrels in the same small cage. In growing old, I find myself strongly preferring the simple and the natural, in men and women as in other aspects of life and art. It is a mistake to suppose that they are stupid; they may not shine in dialectic, but they take notice, and some are very quick indeed. An American woman journalist, addressing American troops in the 'forties on the British Radio, had perceived this. She said: 'Don't worry because English people don't seem to look at you. *They've already looked.*'

I thought this at the time extremely shrewd. The glance of an ordinary man or woman in this country can be devastating. It takes in clothes, manner, expression, and all the little signs of vanity of which the individual is unconscious. The whole process, indeed, is equally unconscious; but if I had been in the habit of feeling surprise I should often have been astonished at the accuracy of judgment I have found in this village during the last forty-five years.

I attribute the accuracy to what some may call a restriction of outlook, which is really a freedom from complexity. The townsman has too many things in his head at the same time. So has the townswoman in hers. Most of these things are irrelevant, although they can give a high polish or delicious association of impulses from which the subtle draw great satisfaction. Accepting the satisfaction, I agree with D. H. Lawrence when he said 'I do like plain outspokenness'; but that is because while (as this book has shown) I am full of vanity, I am, like the countryman, free from intellectual conceit. Down with intellectual conceit! It brings death to the sympathetic imagination!

How much better it is to live in tranquillity and cultivate one's garden. To look out of a window every morning upon lawn and border, and to follow the seasons as each of them brings its own beauty and reward for labour. To see, as Winter hardens the ground, the first peeping of daffodil growth, the odd emergence backward of the aconites, and thenceforward to perceive the early signs of Spring and the gradual re-shaping of plants as they bring colour everywhere; first the yellows of crocus and primrose, the blue of scyllas, the golden glow of alyssum and fine big-trumpeted daffs, the white of arabis, the exquisite pink masses of milkmaids, the crimson tulips (not forgetting their little scarlet brothers, the Fusiliers), and the successive blossoms of plum, cherry, pear, and apple until at last the full glory of roses arrives to glorify the whole year.

I am not trying to list the flowers in detail; for to do this would be impossible. I give the samples as they occur to me, my object being to show that even after one's personal hopes for the future decline through fruition or exhaustion they can be more impersonally revived in the year's procession of beauty. The writer, as a young man, dreams of perfecting his art, or producing some one book which will satisfy his modest ambition. If, like myself, he lives long, and looks with chagrin at an ever-increasing accumulation of titles, each one of which has in its day held the excitement of performance, he cannot suppose that what he will do in future will bring any greater satisfaction. He might well (I do not) feel despair at having achieved so little. He has seen the reputation of other writers shoot into importance and subside; he can never say, with

Swift, 'what a genius I had when I wrote that book!' or believe that anything he has published will outlast his lifetime; but he can feel thankfulness, as I do, for the maintenance of his strength and all the kindness he has received and continues to receive. More is denied him.

As he surveys the garden, however, he is a very Alexander Selkirk. He is monarch of all he surveys. His delights are all in things outside himself. He rejoices in the sunshine and, more temperately, the rain; even the snow, and certainly the wonderful spread of an oak's bare branches and the changing hue of beech and sycamore. Around my studio, every year, arises the brilliant little song of hedge-warbler and wren, which I never hear without marvelling pleasure. In front of the cottage, and in the hedges by the back door, there is a constant coming and going of birds, all of which are busy with plans for the day, with mating, nesting, the feeding of young, and, in due course, the cat-braving assembly of cheeping youngsters who, before agreeing to feed themselves, torment their fathers and mothers into a state of ruffled middle-age. All is a process, the observation of which is absorbing and full of abiding joy.

This is an emotion largely denied the sophisticates, who 'have no time to stand and stare', who must frantically keep up with fashion, stimulate jaded appetites with aphrodisiacs, and relieve a sense of futility by despising the innocent and the good. The innocent and the good laugh last. They live longer, and more richly.

NINE

Passing of
a Village

I F T H E last chapter had a slightly melancholy, or defiant note, as if I were determined to say good words before I too 'into the Dust descend', there was a reason. It will be remembered—perhaps you have forgotten?—that in the beginning of this book I spoke of arriving in the village, and seeing its charm with the hungry eyes of a town-dweller. Well, all I then said was true, and those early days hold memories which are still fragrant; but forty-five years have passed since my wife and I first entered into our home.

They have been forty-five years of united happiness, marred only by the unnecessary loss of our first daughter and the deaths of many beloved friends, of whom I have named but a few. We have had almost unbroken health, our troubles in this regard being confined to small breakages of bones or ligaments; we have seen a second daughter grow from enchanting babyhood to a maturity of charm and assurance; and we have added cordial friends to the older who survive.

That the older ones do survive, and keep their freshness of mind, is one of the alleviations of age. No conversational pleasure known to me at the present time can surpass that which I enjoy with certain old men—as examples, Martin Secker (87) and Compton Mackenzie (86)—whose experience and power to compare like with like over the greater part of a century seems inexhaustible. A common preoccupation with the world of letters is the bond. We never ask 'do you remember?'; memory is taken for granted. And one thing, as the song said, leads to another. Our differences in taste and temperament are minimised; and indeed with Mackenzie and Secker intimacy has been close for so long as to be almost brotherly. We sit relishing our exchanges, still with active minds in which amusement is paramount; and the people we have known swim naturally into view again. We do not envy them, for they are dead. Whatever disabilities we at other times suffer (and my own have no significance), are forgotten. We are content, and do not want to part. There is perhaps a sadness in this reluctance, which arises from a sense that time is our enemy. It was otherwise in youth, when the years ahead were countless, and our contemporaries, now departed, were as full of hope as ourselves. We all first met before the outbreak of calamity in 1914:

'Bliss was it in that dawn to be alive,
But to be young was very heaven.'

Or so, in retrospect, it seems.

My thoughts have taken a mortuary turn, not in relation to these ageing friends, but because my wife and I, as I write, have just returned from a service following the death of a much younger man. One of the first to call at the cottage was a quiet, pale visitor who announced that he had come to collect 'the oldest tax in England'. This, I think, was the Land Tax; and the Collector was a Clerk to the Parish Council who preceded in this office my jovial 'twin' and neighbour, the present holder of it.

He was an extremely pleasant man, who entered at once into

friendly conversation, telling me that his son, a great reader, had been thrilled by the arrival in the village of a real author. The son, it proved, was so great a sufferer from rheumatoid arthritis that he was entirely confined, as a result of illness since the age of sixteen, to bed or a spinal carriage. Finding that it would give him pleasure to talk to me, I suggested that he should be brought down for tea one day; and we discovered that by an arrangement of boards and bricks he could be wheeled right into the studio, there to be propped up with pillows into a half-sitting position and supplied with cakes, tea, and cigarettes.

The boy's great enthusiasm was for Edgar Wallace, whom I slightly knew and admired as a man of great journalistic experience who regarded the writing of books as a legitimate form of enterprise. We spoke of Wallace, Phillips Oppenheim, and other extremely popular authors; and it appeared that there was in the village a well-meaning but mistaken fellow, an excellent amateur painter, whose admiration for Middleton Murry, Katherine Mansfield, and their idols, Dostoevsky, Stendhal, and Chekhov, had caused him to undertake the improvement of our visitor's taste. The consequence was that he had aroused a great resistance to these authors in a mind not attuned to them.

I, although a devotee of Chekhov, as I had been earlier of Dostoevsky and Stendhal, was warned. I made no recommendations whatever. I did no more than offer to lend any books, by any authors, in my possession. The visitor could see them ranged about the walls of the studio. Finding that I was not an intellectual bully or purist, he examined some of the volumes, and at last took away about a dozen. At his next visit he returned them, and took away others; and so continued year after year.

His father died. It was a sorrow; but it did not bring his visits and borrowings to an end. He was wheeled here thereafter by a woman friend who had been at school with him and who, with her sister, showed untiring kindness to both the cripple and his mother. She was, and is, one of the liveliest young women I

189

have ever met, frank, laughing, shrewd, and full of practical knowledge. We made friends with her at once, and regard her with great affection. She did not borrow books; but month after month pushed that heavy carriage through the village for a distance of over a mile each way.

The boy grew older. He learned a great deal from reading, taught himself Dutch and Italian (being helped in the latter by an expert living three miles away in the same village as Philip Gibbs), added Jane Austen, Mrs Gaskell and other novelists to his fervent enthusiasms, and developed a really wide knowledge of English literature. Not only English; for his discovery of Continental authors proceeded apace, and one of his revelations was Thucydides. He borrowed all sorts of books, always because he wanted to read them; and although he passed the age of sixty in the forty-odd years of our acquaintance he remained exactly as he had been at our first meeting.

Alas, his mother died. He was moved, with great considerateness on the part of doctors, the Chairman of the Parish Council, and other well-wishers, to a hospital nine miles away, where he found a new variety of happiness among others, usually much older than himself, who were also permanently disabled. And then, last week, we heard that he was dead. His courage, I am sure, was unbroken to the end, although he refused to borrow any more books, in case they were lost. But for ourselves the loss is considerable, and very saddening. Another link with the village as we first knew it was broken.

I say another link was broken; but indeed the survey of forty-four years shows what changes have occurred in our lives. We have learned to adapt our hearing to the constant passage of peaceable aeroplanes overhead, and our eyes to the sight of them as brilliant streaks flashing across an azure sky or as blinking red signals to local airfields in the darkness. We have ourselves travelled by air over the district by day and night, and though we cannot identify individual planes the experiences have heightened our speculative interest in their destinations.

Where, we wonder, is this one bound? To Gibraltar, Tangier, Nairobi? The names at least of distant places retain their romance, even if the airfields, whether in Glasgow, Athens, or Constantinople, look much alike; and as we do not know these airfields we can believe that each of them has its own beautiful surroundings. It is held out to us as a prospect that we may in time see the further side of the world, as our daughter has done; and we occasionally toy with this notion, only to decide that for the present home life has certain advantages. Home life? But the world itself is changing every minute, growing smaller and more threatening as the days pass.

Not only the larger world but the small section of the world which is immediately about us. Of late years developers have arrived in the village. This is a part of a great scheme to cover a hitherto unspoiled region with many hundreds of new houses; and we are to become, willy-nilly, a community of twelve or fifteen thousand people. As the railway lines have been removed, all new residents will be dependent for transport upon road vehicles. The journey to London, which formerly took an hour, has become at best one of an hour and a half, and the homeward journey frequently takes longer than that. For the elderly, therefore, a visit to London has become an exhausting enterprise. It is a good fifteen years since I last drove our car all the way to town and back, and while we have been driven since then we find the traffic intimidating. As for public transport, one friend, resident thirty miles nearer London, and well-used to ranging the world in search of literary material, announces that it is harder to reach our door than it is to visit Cairo and the Pyramids.

Nevertheless, it would be false to say that the village—it is still referred to as 'the village'—is remote from civilisation. We have our own Cinema; a fine Village Hall, with good acoustics, where public meetings, flower shows, and the local W.I. and Darby and Joan Clubs are accommodated. An excellent book shop, a Public School, and the first of several municipally-directed boarding schools, are supplemented by our own primary and secondary schools and a prosperous branch of the County Library. Words such as 'progress' and 'amenities' are heard all around. There is to be a new Swimming Pool; there is already an elaborate new Shopping Centre; meetings are held to welcome newcomers; and old residents, disliking all change, shake their heads at the passing of what was once a rural, meadow-surrounded home for the few.

The village has desperate traffic problems. It is painted from end to end with double yellow 'no parking' lines. Incomprehensible little tablets have appeared, bearing the words 'At any time', which always remind me of the title of a play, *Never on Sundays*. From exactly four o'clock in the morning until well after midnight on every day of the week, motor vehicles, ranging from lorries, milk-floats, and horse-boxes to mini-cars, omnibuses, and immoderately noisy motor-cycles, flow north and south, east and west. At what traffic quidnuncs call 'peak-hours' the number of these vehicles, driven with the *élan* of those who take pride in new possessions, and much too close upon each other's rear wheels and bumpers, is so great that pedestrians, dogs, cats, reckless sparrows and blackbirds, and slowly purposeful hedgehogs run appalling risks.

Elderly ladies, that incalculable breed, make nothing of such risks. Smiling complacently (as it appears, though the smiles may in fact be placatory), they step directly in front of advancing cars as if they were armour-plated. They are deaf to the motorist's horn; they are beyond reach of his imprecations. As so few of them are knocked down they must enjoy some curious immunity; but there are times when grim drivers, bent upon reaching the coast in twenty minutes, and seemingly unaware that an automobile is a mass of metal capable of smashing human bones and brains as well as posts or crates or tin cans, miss them by the breadth of a whisker.

What with one thing and another, driving in the village is full of hazards. This is admitted by all who have driven without mishap along the great highways of England, through the crowded streets of London, and on the Continent. Not only do elderly ladies dart or stroll, but cars stop suddenly without signal (it may be because their drivers are seeking to avoid pedestrians), debouch at speed from side turnings, try to pass when there is no room to pass, or rush like lemmings to self-destruction at the crossroads. I do not remember whether lemmings screech their horns; the madcap drivers of colliding cars certainly do—their horns and their brakes. With eyes fixed, they model themselves upon Mr Toad, in *The Wind in the Willows*, and escape death and homicide by miracle.

These details will show what changes have come upon the village in less than half-a-century. Where formerly there was a delicious silence, and bricklayers, as I have said, walked ten miles to a job, there is noise at all times, and coaches pass the cottage before seven o'clock each morning on their way to collect bricklayers and others for work, picking them up and dropping them again at their own doors in the evening. Other coaches, an hour or so later, call for schoolchildren who would otherwise be killed on the roads; and at teatime carry them back in a boisterous mass. Schoolchildren abound. A couple of years ago a miniature Brand's Hatch established itself outside our front gate, when boys with new motor-cycles gathered to show their treasures to friends and gave these same friends trips to the village and back every few minutes. Unearthly green street lighting has appeared along the high road, and is still there, and necessary, at one o'clock in the morning. From half-past four in the afternoon, crossing that main road, especially on dusky evenings, when eagle-eyed men drive, as my W.V.S. chauffeuses did during the War, on sidelights only, is a test for nerves. At night heavy transport planes sound like whole fleets of bombers.

The changes, fortunately, have not come all at once. Many arose in the stress of wartime; others have followed a world-pattern and are with us as a part of the national urbanisation.

193

To an older person, such as myself, who dreamed of rural peace, the substitution of noise and speed for tranquillity is unwelcome. We are told we must lead the world in technology; but to me the cry of 'technological know-how' is just as unpleasant as the words 'conurbation' and 'balance of payments', or 'euphoria' and 'psychedelic'. I cannot wonder that social theorists insist upon men ceasing to hold administrative posts after the age of sixty-five.

Even fifty-five, even forty-five, will presently be ages of limit. Quite young men have told me that they find it impossible to keep pace with technical progress in, for instance, medicine and dentistry. They must do the best they can; but the accumulation of new terms and new techniques is so great that the ordinary practitioner, dealing all day long with the oddities and diseases of individual patients, has no time for intensive study. The problem is made more difficult by the jargon in which specialists write.

Here is an example which I cut from *The Guardian* one day in June, 1966. It was there cited by a correspondent from the work of an eminent sociologist who defined the term 'rôle' as 'a sector of the total orientation system of an individual actor which is organised about expectations in relation to a particular interaction context, that is integrated with a particular set of value-standards which govern interaction with one or more alters in the appropriate complementary rôles'.

The same sort of jargon, I know, puts obstacles in the way of would-be students of psychology. Some literary criticism writhes through comparable verbiage. In medicine and philosophy, where every expert defines terms to suit himself and to discourage the lay mind, all is lost. I am entranced by the belief that no such tasks can be expected of me, now or in the future. In the eighties one may remain benignly ignorant, sure that whatever happens in the years of life remaining one can rely on the mercy of all but the most censorious of juniors.

There are many compensations in age. One of them is that

whatever changes there may be elsewhere, and however much the village may extend in other directions, one is attuned to the movement of the age and does not suffer as the young do from anger at the constant narrowings of personal liberty. Strikes are impossible to the writer, who must accept his lot with all possible grace. I am glad not to be a young writer, whose choice of themes, once he has written his autobiographical novel, is restricted; still more glad not to be a middle-aged writer who is out of sympathy with the coming age and sees his prospects darken. I should like to live another ten years, in order to write several books over which I have been brooding for a long time; but I am reconciled to the knowledge that such longevity is improbable. Nor do I regret more than half-a-dozen small mishaps which occurred long ago. To do so would be foolish. 'Since there my past life lies, why alter it?'

Further compensations lie just out of doors. Our village is still far enough from cities to escape the attentions of international crooks and strong-arm gangs. The furies of riot and stabbing lie at a distance. Our football enthusiasts are not wantonly destructive. We have no colour problems, no queues of unemployed, and no lock-outs. I do not think we have ever had a strike; and the only coloured people we see are some charming piccaninnies who are catered for in a large house about a mile away.

The villagers, although augmented in numbers, remain as pleasant as ever in their manners. The shopkeepers, perhaps because we are old residents, greet us with smiles and—this is very important for domestic comfort—supply goods of excellent quality. When, last year, a complete manuscript failed to reach my friend and typist, the whole postal staff was deeply disturbed; and within half an hour of reporting the disaster I received a telephone call from the Postmaster, saying that he had managed to trace the parcel through several other offices, and it was being delivered by hand at once. There is a minimum of snobbery in the village itself. And our worst troubles, apart from traffic and development, are the mounting rates. On the whole this remains a fair corner of England. Furthermore, behind the tall hedges, we enjoy almost the same privacy as before.

It is on this note that I shall end. My trifling excursions in previous chapters have been intended to diversify. They have not represented the concern we feel over much that is happening in the great world, and I have deleted from the manuscript many passages of a controversial nature. I thought them out of place in what was designed as a highly personal book. As a man, and as a writer, I have no complaints to make; and therefore I shall not make them.

Farewell!